A star on the flo[or of] the Rotunda in the United States Capitol marks the point at which Washington, D.C., is divided into four quadrants.

HARCOURT SOCIAL Studies

Exploring Washington, D.C.

Harcourt
SCHOOL PUBLISHERS

www.harcourtschool.com

HARCOURT SOCIAL Studies

Exploring Washington, D.C.

Series Authors

Dr. Michael J. Berson
Professor
Social Science Education
University of South Florida
Tampa, Florida

Dr. Tyrone C. Howard
Associate Professor
UCLA Graduate School of Education &
    Information Studies
University of California at Los Angeles
Los Angeles, California

Dr. Cinthia Salinas
Assistant Professor
Department of Curriculum and
    Instruction
College of Education
The University of Texas at Austin
Austin, Texas

Series Consultants

Dr. Marsha Alibrandi
Assistant Professor of Social Studies
Curriculum and Instruction
    Department
North Carolina State University
Chapel Hill, North Carolina

Dr. Patricia G. Avery
Professor
College of Education and Human
    Development
University of Minnesota
Minneapolis/St. Paul, Minnesota

Dr. Linda Bennett
Associate Professor
College of Education
University of Missouri–Columbia
Columbia, Missouri

Dr. Walter C. Fleming
Department Head and Professor
Native American Studies
Montana State University
Bozeman, Montana

Dr. S. G. Grant
Associate Professor
University at Buffalo
Buffalo, New York

C. C. Herbison
Lecturer
African and African-American Studies
University of Kansas
Lawrence, Kansas

Dr. Eric Johnson
Assistant Professor
Director, Urban Education Program
School of Education
Drake University
Des Moines, Iowa

Dr. Bruce E. Larson
Associate Professor
Social Studies Education
Secondary Education
Woodring College of Education
Western Washington University
Bellingham, Washington

Dr. Merry M. Merryfield
Professor
Social Studies and Global Education
College of Education
The Ohio State University
Columbus, Ohio

Dr. Peter Rees
Associate Professor
Department of Geography
University of Delaware
Wilmington, Delaware

Dr. Phillip J. VanFossen
James F. Ackerman Professor of
    Social Studies Education
Associate Director, Purdue Center for
    Economic Education
Purdue University
West Lafayette, Indiana

Dr. Myra Zarnowski
Professor
Elementary and Early Childhood
    Education
Queens College
The City University of New York
Flushing, New York

Washington, D.C. Consultants

Dr. Lisa Benton-Short
Associate Professor
Department of Geography
The George Washington University
Washington, D.C.

Dr. Maurice Jackson
Assistant Professor
Department of History
Georgetown University
Washington, D.C.

Classroom Reviewers and Contributors

Pamela B. Hayes
Teacher
Neval H. Thomas Elementary
Washington, D.C.

Trina Y. Sheppard
Literacy Coach
Neval H. Thomas Elementary
Washington, D.C.

Angela Sims
Teacher
Marie H. Reed Elementary
Washington, D.C.

Alayne Swimpson
Teacher
Randle Highlands Elementary
Washington, D.C.

Michael W. White
Teacher
Neval H. Thomas Elementary
Washington, D.C.

Blake Yedwab
Teacher
Lafayette Elementary
Washington, D.C.

ISBN-13: 978-0-15-373191-4
ISBN-10: 0-15-373191-5

1 2 3 4 5 6 7 8 9 10 048 15 14 13 12 11 10 09 08 07

Unit 3

The Economy of Washington, D.C.

Unit 4

The History of Washington, D.C.

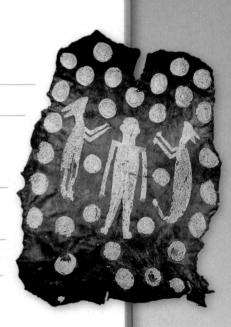

Benjamin Banneker

Black Heritage USA 15c

Features

The Geography of Washington, D.C.

The Big Idea

Land and People

Physical features and human features make Washington, D.C., different from any other place.

What to Know

✔ What are the major physical features of Washington, D.C.?

✔ What kind of human features make each neighborhood in Washington, D.C., different?

✔ What monuments and historical sites help Washington, D.C., stand out as the nation's capital?

continent   One of the seven largest land areas on Earth. (page 5)

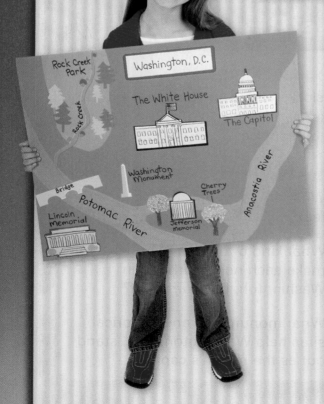

physical feature   A feature of a place's land, water, climate, or plant life. (page 10)

human feature Things that people add to a place. (page 14)

canal A human-made waterway. (page 15)

memorial Something that helps keep the memory of a person or event alive. (page 26)

GO ONLINE For more resources, go to www.harcourtschool.com/ss1

Where Is Washington, D.C.?

What to Know
What are different ways to describe the location of Washington, D.C.?

Vocabulary
continent p. 5
hemisphere p. 5
equator p. 5
relative location p. 6
quadrant p. 7

Main Idea and Details

Your pen pal in Mexico has asked you where you live. What do you say? You could give your street address. You might tell the name of your neighborhood. You might also say that you live north of Mexico. You tell your pen pal that you live in the city of Washington, D.C. Your pen pal writes back, "Where in the world is Washington, D.C.?"

Washington, D.C.'s Location

Illustration Which covers a larger area, North America or the United States?

NORTH AMERICA

PACIFIC OCEAN

ATLANTIC OCEAN

Washington, D.C., in the World

You can say that Washington, D.C., is in the United States. The United States is one of the countries in North America. North America is one of Earth's seven **continents**, or largest land areas.

Hemispheres

You can also name the **hemisphere**, or half of Earth, in which Washington, D.C., is located. Earth is divided into the Northern and Southern Hemispheres by an imaginary line called the **equator**. Washington, D.C., is north of the equator, so it is in the Northern Hemisphere.

Another imaginary line runs from the North Pole to the South Pole. This line divides Earth into the Eastern and Western Hemispheres. North America, the United States, and Washington, D.C., are in the Western Hemisphere.

Reading Check ⚙**Main Idea and Details**
In which hemispheres is Washington, D.C.?

Name: Karina Morgan
Street: 100 Lowell Street, NE
City: Washington, D.C
Country: The United States
Continent: North America

THE UNITED STATES

WASHINGTON, D.C.

Relative Location

"Find Chesapeake Bay on a map of the United States," you write to your pen pal. "My city is just west of it." You go on to explain that Washington, D.C., is between Maryland and Virginia. When you describe your location this way, you are giving your relative location. The **relative location** of a place is where it is in relation to one or more other places on Earth.

Where in the United States?

"In the Mid-Atlantic region" is another way to describe the relative location of Washington, D.C. The city is located in the middle of the Atlantic coast, in a federal district between the states of the Northeast and the states of the Southeast.

Regions of the United States

MAP SKILL **Regions** The United States is divided into five large regions. In which region of the United States is Virginia?

ALASKA

WEST

MIDWEST

NORTHEAST

SOUTHWEST

SOUTHEAST

WASHINGTON, D.C.

HAWAII

Where in the City?

Addresses in Washington, D.C., tell where you are in relation to the United States Capitol. The city has four sections, or **quadrants**. They are Northwest, Northeast, Southeast, and Southwest. They meet at the Capitol. When you are in the Northwest quadrant, you are northwest of the Capitol.

Reading Check ᗄ**Main Idea and Details** Where in the United States is Washington, D.C.?

Summary Washington, D.C., is in the Mid-Atlantic region of the United States, in North America, and in the Northern and Western Hemispheres.

Washington, D.C.'s Four Quadrants

MARYLAND

Rock Creek Park

North Capitol St.

NORTHWEST

NORTHEAST

The Mall | Capitol | East Capitol St.

SOUTH-WEST

Potomac River

South Capitol St.

Anacostia River

SOUTH-EAST

VIRGINIA

MARYLAND

0   2   4 Miles
0   2   4 Kilometers
Albers Equal-Area Projection

MAP SKILL **Regions** Northwest is the largest quadrant in Washington, D.C. Southwest is the smallest. In which quadrant is Rock Creek Park?

Review

1. **What to Know** Where is Washington, D.C., located?

2. **Vocabulary** How are the terms **equator** and **hemisphere** related?

3. **Geography** Which states border Washington, D.C.?

4. **Critical Thinking** Make It Relevant What is the location of your neighborhood relative to the Capitol?

5. **Make a Diagram** Make a diagram with pictures and words to show different ways to give the location of Washington, D.C.

6. **Main Idea and Details** On a sheet of paper, copy and complete the graphic organizer below.

Main Idea

There are several ways to describe the location of Washington, D.C.

Details

Use Latitude and Longitude

Why It Matters Using the lines on maps and globes will help you find a place's location.

❯ Learn

Lines on a map or globe make a grid system. You can use these lines to find the **absolute location**, or exact location, of a place.

Step 1 Find the lines of **latitude**. They run east and west. They measure the distance in degrees (°) north or south of the equator.

Step 2 Find the lines of **longitude**. They run north and south. They measure the degrees east or west of the **prime meridian**.

Step 3 Name the latitude and then the longitude.

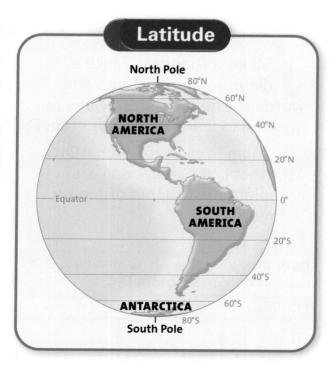

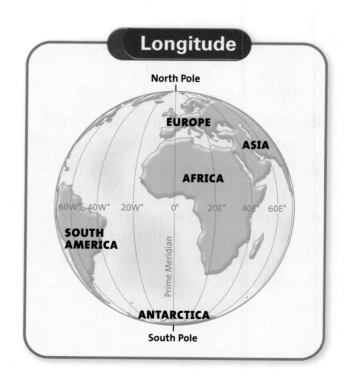

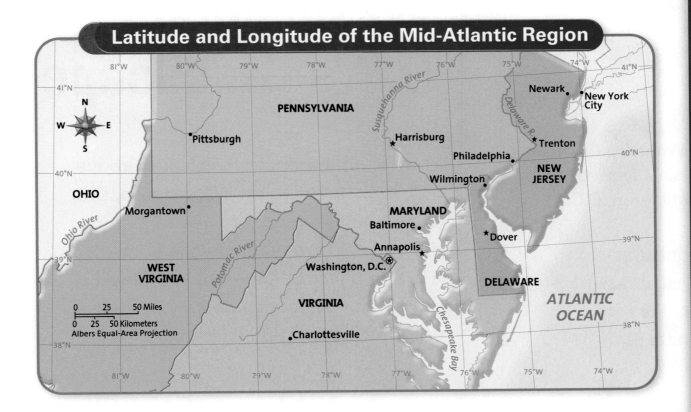

Latitude and Longitude of the Mid-Atlantic Region

❯ Practice

Answer these questions, using the map.

1 What line of longitude runs near Philadelphia?

2 What line of latitude runs nearest to Charlottesville, Virginia?

3 Which city is closest to 74°W longitude?

4 Which city is closest to 39°N, 77°W?

❯ Apply

Make It Relevant Use the map to find the nearest latitude and the nearest longitude of Washington, D.C. Then use a map or a globe to find another city with the same latitude in the United States. Find the longitude for that city. What is the difference in longitude between the other city and Washington, D.C.?

Map and Globe Skills

Washington, D.C.'s Landscape

💡 **What to Know**
What are the main physical features of Washington, D.C.?

Vocabulary
physical feature p. 10
Fall Line p. 11
climate p. 12

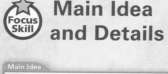
Main Idea and Details

You are an astronaut flying high above Earth, looking down on Washington, D.C. You are much too high to see streets or buildings. Instead, you can see some of the area's physical features. The **physical features** of a place include its waterways, landforms, plants, and climate.

City on the Potomac

From space, the first feature you might see is the Potomac River. People often call Washington, D.C., "the City on the Potomac."

The Potomac flows into Chesapeake Bay. This bay opens into the Atlantic Ocean.

Two smaller bodies of water run through Washington, D.C. Rock Creek and the Anacostia River both feed into the Potomac River.

The Fall Line

Washington, D.C., lies on a line where hilly land at the base of the Appalachian Mountains meets the flat land along the Atlantic Ocean. This line is called the **Fall Line**. Here, rivers drop from higher to lower land. This drop creates waterfalls and rapids. You can see the drop at the Great Falls of the Potomac River northwest of the city.

❯ **Washington, D.C., and the Potomac River as seen from space**

Reading Check 🕹**Main Idea and Details**
What are some waterways in and around Washington, D.C.?

⚡Fast Fact

Native Americans once called the Potomac River *Cohongarooton*, meaning "River of Geese." Many swans and geese lived along the river's banks.

▶ In the spring, cherry trees bloom in Washington, D.C. In the winter, the city can get snow.

Washington, D.C.'s Environment

Climate is another physical feature. **Climate** is the kind of weather a place has over a long time. Like other places in this part of the United States, Washington, D.C., has a mostly warm climate. Summers are hot and humid. Winters are generally mild, but it can snow at times.

Plants and Animals

The climate in Washington D.C., affects the kinds of plants and animals that live there. Oak, magnolia, and sycamore trees grow in the warm climate. The city also is famous for its cherry trees. The trees came from Japan. They grow well in the Washington, D.C., climate, too.

Forest animals such as squirrels, deer, foxes, raccoons, and opossums live in wooded areas in Rock Creek Park, in Fort Du Pont Park, and on Theodore Roosevelt Island. Mockingbirds, blue jays, wood thrushes, and orioles fly about the city.

Reading Check 🔎 **Main Idea and Details**
What kinds of plants and animals live in Washington, D.C.?

Summary Washington, D.C., is on the Potomac River. It sits near the Fall Line, where the land drops from high to low. The climate of Washington, D.C., is hot in the summer. Winters are mostly mild. The climate affects the kinds of plants and animals that live in the area.

❯ Wood thrushes and raccoons are among the wildlife that can be seen in Washington, D.C.

Review

1. **What to Know** What are some physical features in Washington, D.C.?

2. **Vocabulary** Use the term **Fall Line** in a sentence to describe it.

3. **Geography** How does the climate of Washington, D.C., affect the kinds of plants that grow there?

4. **Critical Thinking** Washington, D.C., was built below the Potomac's Great Falls, not above them. Why do you think this was so?

5. **Draw a Map** Draw a map of an area of the city you know well. Include any bodies of water, parks, hills, trees, or other physical features in the area.

6. **Main Idea and Details** On a sheet of paper, copy and complete the graphic organizer below.

Main Idea
The physical features of Washington, D.C., set it apart from other places.

Details

Lesson 3 Washington, D.C.'s Neighborhoods

What to Know

What makes each of Washington, D.C.'s neighborhoods different?

Vocabulary

human feature p. 14

canal p. 15

immigrant p. 17

suburb p. 20

Main Idea and Details

Focus Skill

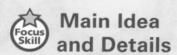

How is your neighborhood different from others? The buildings in your neighborhood might look different from those in another neighborhood. Or there might be different restaurants, shops, and other businesses. The people who live there might come from another country. Also, your neighborhood has its own history. These are all **human features**, things that people add to a place. All of Washington, D.C.'s neighborhoods have their own human features.

Georgetown in 1855

Georgetown

Georgetown, Maryland, was settled in 1751. It was on the land that was selected for the capital city. The town became part of Washington, D.C. It is in the Northwest quadrant of Washington, D.C.

Georgetown became a busy trade port on the Potomac River. It was also on the Chesapeake and Ohio (C&O) Canal. A **canal** is a human-made waterway. By using the canal, ships could sail around the waterfalls on the Potomac River.

After the Civil War, many African Americans settled in Georgetown. Many worked at the port. Later, people from many different backgrounds settled in Georgetown.

Reading Check **Cause and Effect**
What helped Georgetown grow?

❯ How has Georgetown changed over time?

Georgetown in 1865

Georgetown today

More Northwest Neighborhoods

Many more of the oldest neighborhoods in Washington, D.C., are also in the city's Northwest quadrant.

Shaw/U Street

The Shaw/U Street neighborhood was settled by people freed from slavery. It was named for Robert Gould Shaw. He led an all-African American group of soldiers in the Civil War.

In the early 1900s, this neighborhood became a center of African American life. It had restaurants, theaters, and jazz clubs. The Lincoln Theater and the Howard Theater were famous. Howard University is nearby. The neighborhood was one of the first in the city to have an electric streetcar.

▶ **This photograph shows the Shaw/U Street neighborhood in 1950. A mural of Duke Ellington, a famous jazz musician, is a well-known feature of the neighborhood today.**

> You know you are in Chinatown (left) or Adams Morgan (above) when you see these famous landmarks.

Adams Morgan

Adams Morgan is one of the most diverse communities in the city. The neighborhood gets much of its character from the many immigrants who live there. An **immigrant** is a person who has moved from another country to live in this country. People from Africa, Central and South America and other parts of the world make their homes and run their businesses in Adams Morgan. There are many restaurants and shops that have African, Asian, European, and Caribbean meals and goods.

Chinatown

Chinatown was first settled by German immigrants. In the 1930s, many Chinese Americans moved in. Many opened shops, restaurants, and other businesses. All signs in the area are in both Chinese and English.

Reading Check ᕆMain Idea and Details
For what did the Shaw/U Street neighborhood become famous?

Northeast

Brookland is one of the historic neighborhoods in the Northeast quadrant. The area was once a farm. In the late 1800s, Catholic University was built in the area. Soon many Catholics were living in Brookland. In 1920, the Catholic community of Washington, D.C., began building a huge church in Brookland.

Today, Brookland has the nickname "Little Rome." This is because it has more Catholic churches and buildings than any other place outside the Vatican, in Italy.

Deanwood is another neighborhood in the Northeast quadrant that used to be farmland. Many African Americans began moving to the area in the late 1800s. A teacher named Nannie Helen Burroughs opened a boarding school for girls in Deanwood in 1909.

Capitol Hill

Capitol Hill is the largest historic neighborhood in Washington, D.C. It lies between two quadrants—Northeast and Southeast. When the United States government moved to Washington, D.C., in 1800, many government workers settled in the area around the Capitol building. Also, people who worked at the Washington Navy Yard and workers who were helping to build the Capitol moved there. Today, about one-third of the members of Congress live in Capitol Hill.

Reading Check ♥**Main Idea and Details**
Who settled in Brookland and Capitol Hill?

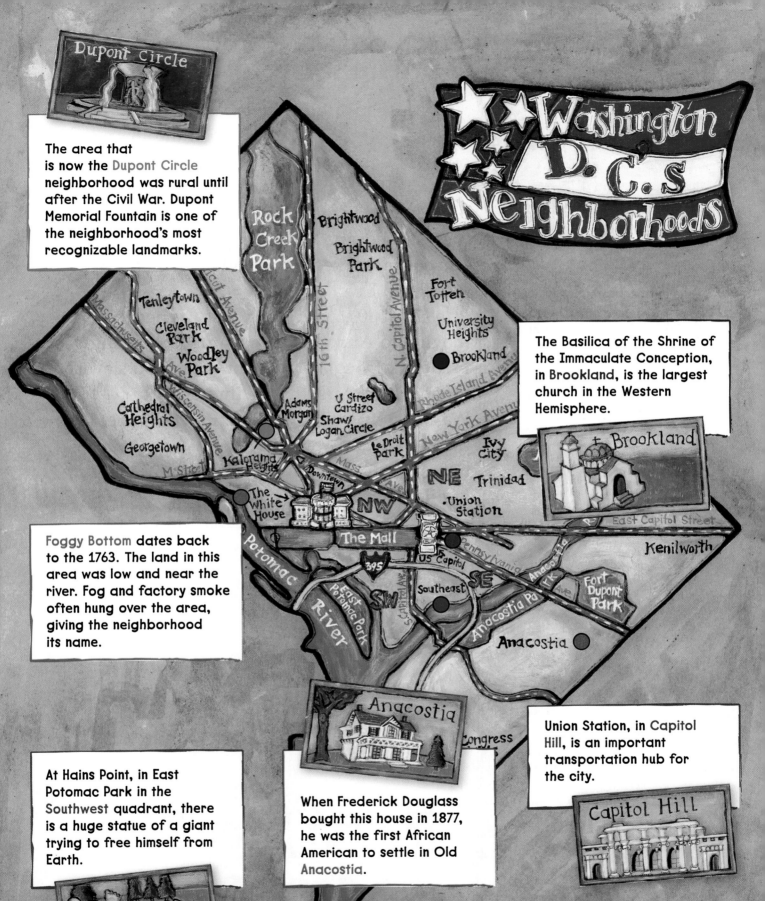

Dupont Circle

The area that is now the Dupont Circle neighborhood was rural until after the Civil War. Dupont Memorial Fountain is one of the neighborhood's most recognizable landmarks.

Washington D.C.'s Neighborhoods

The Basilica of the Shrine of the Immaculate Conception, in Brookland, is the largest church in the Western Hemisphere.

Brookland

Foggy Bottom dates back to the 1763. The land in this area was low and near the river. Fog and factory smoke often hung over the area, giving the neighborhood its name.

Union Station, in Capitol Hill, is an important transportation hub for the city.

Capitol Hill

At Hains Point, in East Potomac Park in the Southwest quadrant, there is a huge statue of a giant trying to free himself from Earth.

Southwest

When Frederick Douglass bought this house in 1877, he was the first African American to settle in Old Anacostia.

Anacostia

Illustration What are some neighborhoods in the Northeast quadrant?

Southeast and Southwest

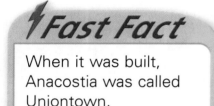

▶ **Visitors to the Anacostia Museum learn about the neighborhood's history.**

Anacostia is in the Southeast quadrant of Washington, D.C. It was built in the 1850s as one of the first suburbs of the city. A **suburb** is a smaller town near a city. In the new suburb, homes were bigger and less expensive than those in the city. Many people who lived in Anacostia worked on the other side of the Anacostia River.

In the 1880s, African Americans began moving to Anacostia. One famous resident was Frederick Douglass. He worked to end slavery.

For many years, the Southwest part of Washington, D.C., was cut off from the rest of the city by the Washington City Canal. From the mid-1800s to the early 1900s, poor working families settled in this waterfront area. Many of them were African Americans and immigrants from Italy, Germany, Scotland, Ireland, and

⚡ ***Fast Fact***

When it was built, Anacostia was called Uniontown.

▶ **Anacostia in the early 1900s**

eastern Europe. Many of them worked on the docks and at the fish markets and other businesses along the riverfront.

Southwest's long history can still be seen today. Some people still make their home in Wheat Row, the oldest group of townhouses in Washington, D.C. People still do business at Southwest's lively fish market, too.

Reading Check ÖMain Idea and Details
What cut off the Southwest quadrant from the rest of the city?

Summary All parts of Washington, D.C., have interesting neighborhoods. Each has its own history and its own character.

➤ Washingtonians can buy fresh seafood from Chesapeake Bay at the Maine Avenue Fish Market, in the Southwest quadrant.

Review

1. **What to Know** What makes each neighborhood in Washington, D.C., different?

2. **Vocabulary** Use the terms **canal** and **suburb** to explain how some neighborhoods are settled.

3. **Culture** How have immigrants affected the character of Adams Morgan?

4. **Critical Thinking** What are some reasons people move to a certain neighborhood?

5. **Interview a Person** Interview a long-time resident of your neighborhood. Ask how the area has changed. Then give a report.

6. **Main Idea and Details** On a sheet of paper, copy and complete the graphic organizer below.

Main Idea

There are interesting neighborhoods in all parts of Washington, D.C.

Details

Compare History Maps

Why It Matters Comparing maps of an area from different times helps you see how the area has changed and how it has stayed the same.

❯ Learn

A **history map** shows you how a place looked during an earlier time period.

Step 1 Look at the first map. It shows the land that became Washington, D.C., in 1792. Then look at the second map. It shows the city in 1886.

Step 2 Compare the two maps. What features are the same? What features are different?

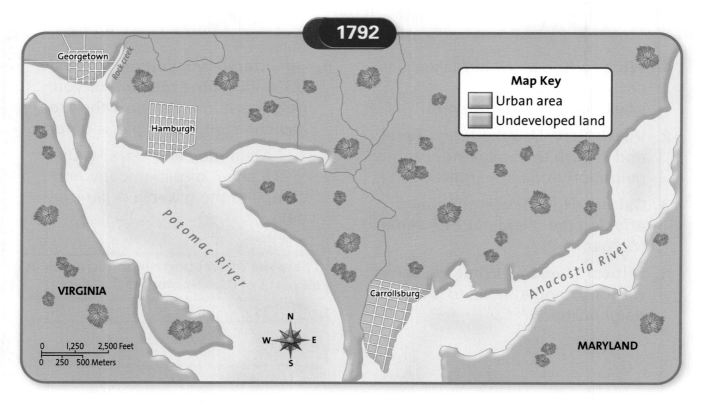

1792

Georgetown

Rock Creek

Hamburgh

Map Key
Urban area
Undeveloped land

Potomac River

Anacostia River

VIRGINIA

Carrollsburg

N
W   E
S

MARYLAND

0   1,250   2,500 Feet
0   250 500 Meters

❱ Practice

Look carefully at the two maps. Examine the titles and map keys. Then answer the following questions.

1 What neighborhood is shown on both maps?

2 What waterways are shown on the 1886 map but not on the 1792 map?

3 What new human features appear on the Potomac River on the 1886 map?

❱ Apply

Make It Relevant Compare both maps to a map of Washington, D.C., today. List features that have changed and features that have not changed. Then compare your list with that of a partner.

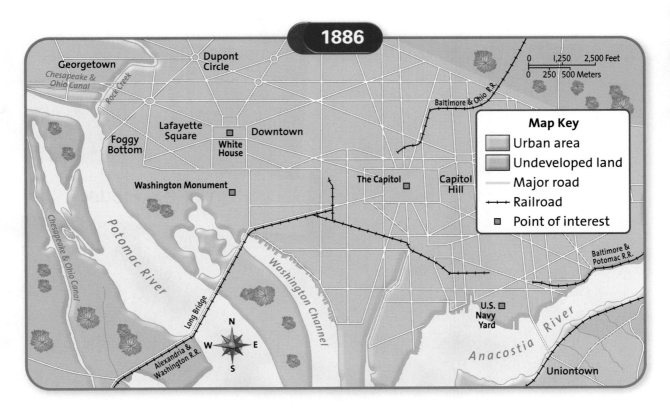

1886

Map Key
- Urban area
- Undeveloped land
- Major road
- Railroad
- Point of interest

Map and Globe Skills

Lesson **4**

Places to See in Washington, D.C.

What to Know

What kinds of important places are there to see in Washington, D.C.?

Vocabulary

monument p. 26

memorial p. 26

veteran p. 26

Main Idea and Details

You are designing a brand-new capital city for our nation. People from around the world will visit. The city will show them what is most important to the nation's people. It should remind the people of the nation's history and purpose. Its symbols should make the people proud. What should the city look like? What places would you include?

White House

Government Buildings

The leaders of the United States run the country from Washington, D.C. The White House, on Pennsylvania Avenue, is where the President lives and works. At the center of the city is the United States Capitol. This building is where Congress meets to make the country's laws. In the Supreme Court Building, judges make sure that the laws are fair.

The government keeps books, documents, and other records that are important to our country's history. Many of them are kept at the Library of Congress and at the National Archives. At the National Archives, people can see two of the nation's most important documents—the Declaration of Independence and the Constitution.

⚡Fast Fact

The Library of Congress is the world's largest library. It has more than 500 miles of shelves that contain more than 100 million publications.

Reading Check 📙 **Main Idea and Details**
What are some important government buildings in Washington, D.C.?

National Archives

Jefferson Memorial

National Zoological Park

Monuments and Memorials

The Washington, D.C., landscape is dotted with monuments. A **monument** is a structure built to honor an important person or event. It can be a building, a pillar, or a statue. Some monuments are also memorials. A **memorial** helps keep the memory of a person or an event alive.

Honoring Presidents

Many of the city's monuments and memorials honor Presidents. The Washington Monument honors our first President, George Washington.

The Jefferson Memorial honors President Thomas Jefferson, who helped write the Declaration of Independence. The Lincoln Memorial honors the life and work of President Abraham Lincoln. Another memorial honors President Franklin Delano Roosevelt.

War Memorials

Some memorials in Washington, D.C., help people remember the soldiers who fought in wars. They include the National World War II Memorial, the Korean War Veterans Memorial, and the Vietnam Veterans Memorial. A **veteran** is a person who fought in a war.

Across the Potomac River, in Virginia, is the Iwo Jima (EE•woh JEE•muh) Memorial. It honors soldiers who fought a famous battle in World War II. Nearby is Arlington National Cemetery. Many soldiers who died in battle are buried there.

VIETNAM VETERANS MEMORIAL

(Reading Check) ᛔMain Idea and Details
Whom do the city's memorials honor?

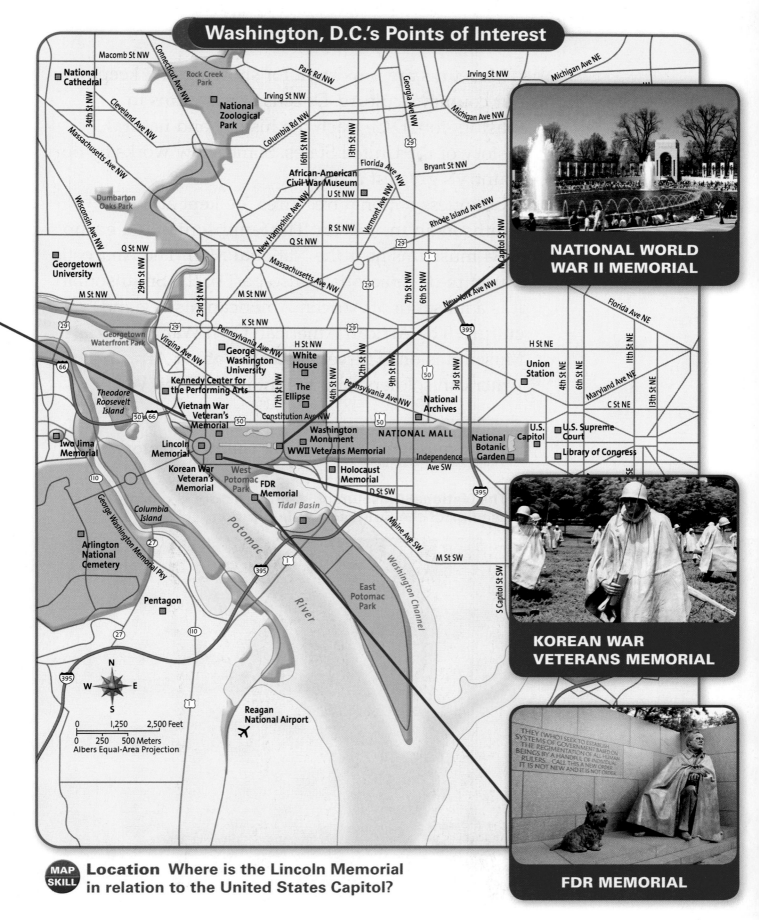

Washington, D.C.'s Points of Interest

Macomb St NW
National Cathedral
34th St NW
Massachusetts Ave NW
Cleveland Ave NW
Rock Creek Park
Connecticut Ave NW
Park Rd NW
Irving St NW
National Zoological Park
Columbia Rd NW
16th St NW
13th St NW
Georgia Ave NW
Irving St NW
Michigan Ave NE
Michigan Ave NW
29
Florida Ave NW
Bryant St NW
African-American Civil War Museum
U St NW
Vermont Ave NW
New Hampshire Ave NW
Rhode Island Ave NW
N Capitol St NW
Wisconsin Ave NW
Dumbarton Oaks Park
Q St NW
R St NW
Q St NW
29
29
Georgetown University
29th St NW
Massachusetts Ave NW
29
M St NW
M St NW
7th St NW
6th St NW
New York Ave NW
1
NATIONAL WORLD WAR II MEMORIAL
Florida Ave NE
66
Georgetown Waterfront Park
29
23rd St NW
K St NW
Pennsylvania Ave NW
29
H St NW
395
H St NE
Union Station
4th St NE
6th St NE
Maryland Ave NE
11th St NE
13th St NE
Virginia Ave NW
George Washington University
George Washington University
White House
12th St NW
9th St NW
3rd St NW
50
C St NE
Theodore Roosevelt Island
Kennedy Center for the Performing Arts
17th St NW
The Ellipse
Pennsylvania Ave NW
National Archives
National Botanic Garden
U.S. Capitol
U.S. Supreme Court
Library of Congress
50 66
Vietnam War Veteran's Memorial
50
14th St NW
Constitution Ave NW
Washington Monument
WWII Veterans Memorial
NATIONAL MALL
Iwo Jima Memorial
Lincoln Memorial
Independence Ave SW
Korean War Veteran's Memorial
West Potomac Park
Holocaust Memorial
395
110
FDR Memorial
D St SW
S Capitol St SW
KOREAN WAR VETERANS MEMORIAL
Columbia Island
Tidal Basin
Potomac
Maine Ave SW
M St SW
George Washington Memorial Pky
27
Arlington National Cemetery
River
East Potomac Park
Washington Channel
395
Pentagon
110
1
27
110
395
N
W E
S
0   1,250   2,500 Feet
0   250   500 Meters
Albers Equal-Area Projection
Reagan National Airport
1
THEY (WHO) SEEK TO ESTABLISH SYSTEMS OF GOVERNMENT BASED ON THE REGIMENTATION OF ALL HUMAN BEINGS BY A HANDFUL OF INDIVIDUAL RULERS . . . CALL THIS A NEW ORDER. IT IS NOT NEW AND IT IS NOT ORDER.

FDR MEMORIAL

MAP SKILL **Location** Where is the Lincoln Memorial in relation to the United States Capitol?

Museums

Museums are important for showing and keeping our country's culture. Dozens of museums in Washington, D.C., teach the history and natural history of the United States. Some show works by our country's greatest artists.

Countless national treasures are kept at the Smithsonian Institution. The Smithsonian is a group of 14 museums near the National Mall. The Anacostia Museum in Anacostia is also part of the Smithsonian. It is a museum of African American history and culture. The African American Civil War Memorial Museum is on U Street. It teaches about African American soldiers who fought in the Civil War.

Reading Check ☼**Generalize**
How do museums preserve our country's history?

❯ **The National Museum of Natural History is one of the museums of the Smithsonian Institution.**

Historical Sites

Many other places in Washington, D.C., have had an important role in United States history. Some of these places are homes of great leaders. The Mary McLeod Bethune Council House honors a leader in education for African American women. The Frederick Douglass National Historic Site in Anacostia honors another great leader. Mount Vernon, in nearby Virginia, was the home of George Washington.

Reading Check ♻**Main Idea and Details**
What are some historical sites in Washington, D.C?

Summary The many government buildings, monuments, and museums in Washington, D.C., are reminders of our nation's history and purpose.

❯ The Mary McLeod Bethune Council House, on Vermont Avenue, was the headquarters for the National Council of Negro Women.

Review

1. **What to Know** What kinds of important places are there to see in Washington, D.C.?

2. **Vocabulary** How are the terms **monument** and **memorial** related?

3. **Civics and Government** Why does Washington, D.C., have so many government buildings?

4. **Critical Thinking** Why is it important to remember people and events from the past?

5. **Create a Guide** Choose a monument. Create a guide for tourists. Include a drawing of the monument. Explain why it is important.

6. **Main Idea and Details** On a sheet of paper, copy and complete the graphic organizer below.

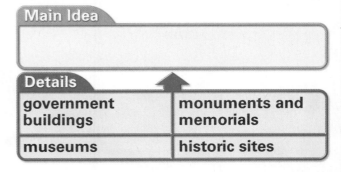

Main Idea	

Details	
government buildings	monuments and memorials
museums	historic sites

FIELD TRIP

READ ABOUT

The National Mall is sometimes called "the nation's front yard." This open space in the heart of Washington, D.C., was designed to be a gathering place for all Americans. People come here to learn about the great leaders and important events in the nation's history.

Around the Mall are monuments to the founders of American democracy. There are also the museums of the Smithsonian Institution.

The Mall is often the site of celebrations. For example, people come to the Mall to celebrate Independence Day. They have picnics and watch fireworks. The Mall has also been a place for protest marches.

FIND

WASHINGTON, D.C.

The National Mall

The National Mall

The Smithsonian Kite Festival is one of the most popular events on the Mall.

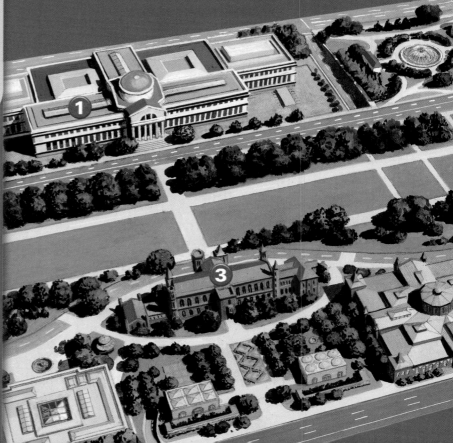

National Museum of Natural History

National Gallery of Art

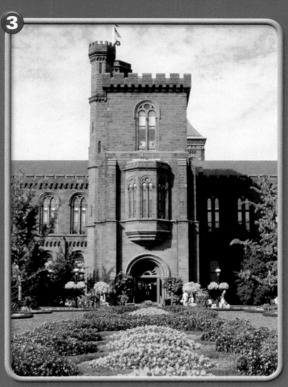

Smithsonian Castle

National Air and Space Museum

National Museum of the American Indian

A VIRTUAL TOUR

GO ONLINE For more resources go to
www.harcourtschool.com/ss1

Visual Summary

The physical features of Washington, D.C., include bodies of water.

Summarize the Unit

Main Idea and Details Complete the graphic organizer to show that you understand the main idea and details about the geography of Washington, D.C.

Main Idea

Its location, physical features, and human features make Washington, D.C. different from other communities.

Details

Vocabulary

Write the correct term from the list to complete each sentence.

1. A _____ is where something is in relation to other places.

2. Waterways, landforms, and climate are _____ of a place.

3. People often work in a city but live in a _____.

4. A _____ helps keep the memory of a person alive.

5. Streets, buildings, bridges, and canals are _____ of a place.

Word Bank

relative location p. 6

physical features p. 10

human features p. 14

suburb p. 20

memorial p. 26

Human features also make up the character of Washington, D.C.

The city has many monuments, memorials, and museums.

 Facts and Main Ideas

Answer these questions.

6. Where in the United States is Washington, D.C.?

7. What waterways are in or near Washington, D.C?

8. What is the climate like in Washington, D.C.?

9. How is Chinatown different from other neighborhoods in Washington, D.C.?

Write the letter of the best choice.

10. Which of the following is a human feature of Washington, D.C.?
    A the Great Falls of the Potomac
    B its relative location
    C the Fall Line
    D the C&O Canal

11. What town was within the boundaries of Washington, D.C., when it was settled?
    A Georgetown
    B Adams Morgan
    C Brookland
    D Chinatown

 Critical Thinking

12. **Make It Relevant** What are three human features of your neighborhood?

13. How can remembering the past affect the future?

 Skills

Compare History Maps

14. Study the maps on pages 22 and 23. List two changes in human features and physical features from 1792 to 1886.

writing

✎ **Write a Report** Research and write a report about a monument or historical site in Washington, D.C. Tell why the place is important.

✎ **Write a Journal** Write a journal entry describing the city's monuments as if you are seeing them for the first time. Tell how they make you feel.

Fun with Social Studies

Terrific Travels

Which picture is on the other side of each postcard?

1

Dear Grandma,
I wish you were here to see where the President lives and works. Imagine all the exciting work that happens here!

3

Hi, Sue!
This place is amazing! It is so tall and a great monument to our first President. It takes 70 seconds to ride the elevator all the way to the top!

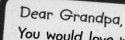

2

Dear Ms. Brown,
Remember when we studied government in class? Today, I am at the place where our leaders make the laws for our country! Its dome is one of the most famous features of a building in the country.

4

Dear Grandpa,
You would love where we are today. This monument helps us remember one of our Presidents, who also helped write the Declaration of Independence. It is a great place!

Government in Washington, D.C.

The Big Idea

Government

Governments provide order and protect rights.

What to Know

- ✓ Why do communities need governments?

- ✓ How does the city government of Washington, D.C., work?

- ✓ How can people influence government?

constitution A plan of government. (page 40)

ambassador A representative to another country. (page 45)

council A group that meets to make laws. (page 50)

municipal Having to do with a city. (page 48)

jury A group of citizens who attend a trial and then decide whether the person on trial has broken a law. (page 57)

GO ONLINE For more resources, go to www.harcourtschool.com/ss1

Lesson 1

Kinds of Government

What to Know
What is the function of government?

Vocabulary
Constitution p. 40
federal p. 40
ambassador p. 45

Focus Skill
Cause and Effect

Cause	Effect

Lately, there have been a lot of traffic accidents at one of the intersections in your neighborhood. You think that a traffic light should be put there. It would make the intersection safer. Whom would a person call to see that this gets done? Someone in the national government, or someone in the city government?

> **What do you think would happen if the government did not fix traffic lights?**

> Police officers help keep people in a community safe.

Why Do We Have Governments?

The main job of government is to make and carry out laws. Laws help people live together in safety and order. They help settle disagreements and unite people.

Governments also protect people's rights and freedoms. For example, government leaders pass laws to make sure all people are treated fairly.

Finally, governments provide services. They provide for our safety, health, and education. They build and repair roads, make sure our drinking water is clean, and help people pay medical bills. As a result, people can stay safe and healthy.

Reading Check ŏ**Cause and Effect**
How does having a government keep order in a community?

A Federal System

The United States **Constitution** is the plan of government for the whole country. It explains how the **federal**, or national, government is organized and what its purpose is. The Constitution gives all the states the right to form their own governments. The states, in turn, allow counties, cities, and towns within their borders to form local governments. The power to govern is shared among the national, state, and local governments.

Each level of government has its own laws and helps people work together to solve problems. Each level of government, however, handles problems of a different size or kind.

❯ The United States Constitution was approved in 1788.

Chart Why do you think each level of government has the power to collect taxes?

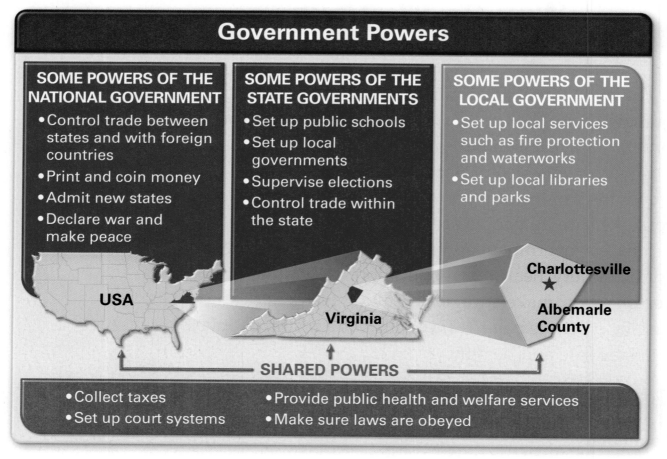

Government Powers

SOME POWERS OF THE NATIONAL GOVERNMENT
- Control trade between states and with foreign countries
- Print and coin money
- Admit new states
- Declare war and make peace

USA

SOME POWERS OF THE STATE GOVERNMENTS
- Set up public schools
- Set up local governments
- Supervise elections
- Control trade within the state

Virginia

SOME POWERS OF THE LOCAL GOVERNMENT
- Set up local services such as fire protection and waterworks
- Set up local libraries and parks

Charlottesville
★
Albemarle County

SHARED POWERS
- Collect taxes
- Set up court systems
- Provide public health and welfare services
- Make sure laws are obeyed

Branches of the Government

	LEGISLATIVE	EXECUTIVE	JUDICIAL
NATIONAL GOVERNMENT	The main body of the legislative branch at the national level is Congress. It makes laws for the whole country. Congress has two parts—the Senate and the House of Representatives.	At the national level, the President is the leader of the executive branch. The President carries out the nation's laws.	The Supreme Court and other federal courts make up the judicial branch at the national level. This branch makes sure national laws are applied fairly.
STATE GOVERNMENT	Each state has a legislature to make laws for the state.	The governor is the head of the executive branch at the state level. The governor carries out the state's laws.	The states also have courts to make sure that state laws are applied fairly.

Table The national and state governments have three parts, or branches. No branch of government is more powerful than any other. Why do you think government has three branches?

National Government

The national government takes care of issues that affect the entire country. It is the job of the national government to protect the freedom of all Americans. It makes sure all Americans are treated fairly. The United States government controls trade and keeps peace with other nations. If necessary, people in the federal government decide to go to war to protect us. It makes coins and money for the whole country to use. The federal government also supports national parks and forests. The postal service is also a part of the federal government.

Reading Check **Main Idea and Details**
What are the three levels of government?

State and Local Governments

State governments make and apply laws for the people of a state. Each state has a constitution that protects the rights of people in the state. State governments build and repair state highways and parks. Also, they make sure that schools in that state provide students with a good education. States also have public colleges and universities.

Like the national government, each state government has three branches. The governor is the head of the executive branch. As a person living near Virginia and Maryland, you might often hear about the governors of those states. Each state also has a legislature to make laws for the state. The state courts and each state's Supreme Court make up the judicial branch.

❯ **You do not live in a state, but your friend in neighboring Virginia or Maryland does.**

The capital of Maryland is Annapolis.

The capital of Virginia is Richmond.

▶ Making sure that young people in Washington, D.C., get a good education is a job of the local government.

Local governments make laws and solve problems for a community. That community may be a county, a town, or a city.

Local governments build and repair local streets. They see to it that traffic lights in the city work properly. Local governments provide fire and police protection in their area. They run public libraries and some museums. They remove snow from the streets and pick up trash. They care for city parks.

Local governments also run public schools in the community. They hire the teachers and take care of the school buildings.

Reading Check ŏ **Cause and Effect**
What effect does city government have on your neighborhood?

> Washington, D.C., Mayor Adrian Fenty (center) meets often with Virginia Governor Jim Kaine (left) and Maryland Governor Martin O'Malley to talk about issues that affect the people of Metropolitan Washington.

Metropolitan Washington Council of Governments

MARYLAND

WEST VIRGINIA

FREDERICK COUNTY
Frederick

Potomac River

0   10   20 Miles
0   10   20 Kilometers

Gaithersburg
MONTGOMERY COUNTY
LOUDOUN COUNTY
Rockville
Takoma Park • Greenbelt
Falls Church • College Park
Fairfax • ⊛Washington, D.C.
FAIRFAX COUNTY Alexandria
PRINCE WILLIAM COUNTY
PRINCE GEORGES COUNTY
VIRGINIA

Chesapeake Bay

N W E S

MAP SKILL Regions What Maryland counties are part of the Metropolitan Washington Council of Governments?

Governments Work Together

Different levels of government often work together to solve certain problems. Leaders in Washington, D.C., and in cities and counties in neighboring Maryland and Virginia work together. They work to solve problems that affect all the people in the region. Leaders at the state, county, and city levels of government formed the Metropolitan Washington Council of Governments (COG). The group works to find solutions to transportation, health, and environmental problems in the region.

Our national government also works with the governments of other nations. The United States sends representatives, called **ambassadors**, to their capital cities. Other nations send their ambassadors to Washington, D.C. The ambassadors of many nations have offices in Washington, D.C. Many of their offices are on or near Massachusetts Avenue.

Reading Check ŏMain Idea and Details
In what ways do different levels of government work together?

Summary The job of government is to keep order, protect rights, and provide services. There are three levels of government in the United States: national, state, and local. All levels work together to solve problems.

❯ **Ambassadors in Washington, D.C., work with United States leaders.**

Review

1. **What to Know** Why do communities need a government?

2. **Vocabulary** How are the terms **federal** and **Constitution** related?

3. **Civics and Government** How do governments protect the rights of citizens in a community?

4. **Civics and Government** What is the job of each branch of government?

5. **Critical Thinking** Why do different levels of government solve different problems?

6. **Create a Poster** Make a poster that shows three ways the government keeps order and three ways it protects people's rights.

7. **Cause and Effect** On a sheet of paper, copy and complete the graphic organizer below.

Cause	Effect
Governments make laws to keep order.	

Cause	Effect
	People are safe and healthy.

FIELD TRIP

THE WHITE HOUSE

READ ABOUT

The President lives and works at the White House, at 1600 Pennsylvania Avenue. It is a symbol of the United States government.

The President and the First Family live in the middle section of the White House. This section has 6 floors, 132 rooms, and 35 bathrooms. A large dining room can serve 140 guests.

The East and West Wings were added in the early 1900s. The President works in the West Wing, in the Oval Office. The First Lady's office is in the East Wing. Hundreds of other people work at the White House every day, helping the President run the country.

FIND

WASHINGTON, D.C.

The White House

Some children of Presidents have called the White House home. John F. Kennedy, Jr. played in the Oval Office.

To save money during World War I, sheep were used to keep the grass on the White House lawn short. Sheep were used to nibble at the grass.

The White House library

In the Situation Room

The President at work in the Oval Office

The White House dining room

A VIRTUAL TOUR

GO ONLINE For more resources go to www.harcourtshool.com/ss1

Lesson 2

Washington, D.C., Government

What to Know
How does the city government of Washington, D.C., work?

Vocabulary
municipal p. 48
council p. 50
commission p. 51

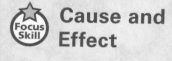

Cause and Effect
Focus Skill

The government of Washington, D.C., is unlike any other local government. The city is not part of any state. It is a federal district. The District of Columbia was created to contain the capital city of the United States.

A Unique Government

Washington, D.C., has a **municipal** (myoo•NIH•suh•puhl), or city, government. But the city is also under the control of the federal government. Many of the decisions made by the city leaders have to be approved by the United States Congress. This is not true for other cities.

Fast Fact

Washington, D.C.'s official symbols include a district flag, a seal, a bird, and a flower. In 2006, 5th and 6th graders from Anthony Bowen Elementary School proposed that the cherry should be Washington, D.C.'s official fruit.

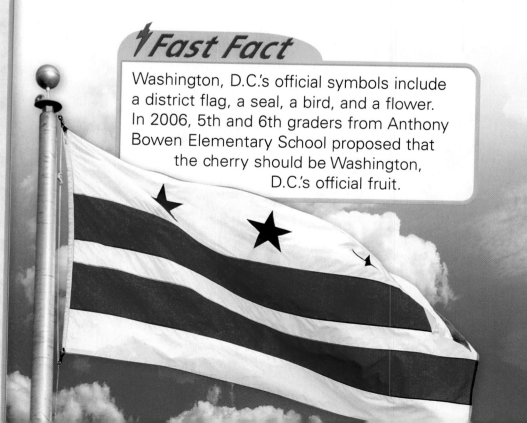

The Seal of Washington, D.C.

Background The seal of the District of Columbia is used on all official city papers.

The figure placing a wreath on the statue stands for justice. Her blindfold shows that justice should be blind, so that it treats everyone the same.

DISTRICT OF COLUMBIA

Statue of George Washington

DBQ Document-Based Question What is the building that is shown on the seal?

The job of the mayor of Washington, D.C., is like that of the mayors of other cities. But because Washington, D.C., is not part of any state, its mayor is in some ways also like the governor of a state.

Washington, D.C., is different from the states in another way. The people who live there do not have all the same rights as people who live in a state. They can elect only a single member to the House of Representatives. This person cannot vote on any laws.

Some people want the District of Columbia to be a state. That way, the people there would have the same rights that people outside Washington, D.C., have. If it should become a state, some people would like it to be called New Columbia.

▶ **Eleanor Holmes Norton has been Washington, D.C.'s representative in Congress since 1991.**

Reading Check ⏱ **Cause and Effect**
How does being a federal district affect the kind of government Washington, D.C., has?

District of Columbia Wards

MARYLAND

VIRGINIA

0   2   4 Miles
0   2   4 Kilometers

N
W   E
S

Rock Creek

Potomac River

Anacostia River

MARYLAND

4
3
1
5
2
6
7
8

Map Key
— Neighborhood boundary

MAP SKILL **Regions** Washington, D.C., is divided into eight wards. In which ward is your neighborhood?

Running the City

Like the federal and state governments, the Washington, D.C., city government has three branches. The mayor is the head of the executive branch of the city government. He or she runs the day-to-day activities of the city.

The city council is the legislative branch. A **council** is a group that meets to make laws. Thirteen people serve on the city council. There is one person from each of the city's eight wards, or sections. The other five city council members can come from anywhere in the city.

The city courts make up the judicial branch. Their judges decide whether city laws are fair and whether laws have been broken.

❯ Members of the Washington, D.C., city council

The city has 37 Advisory Neighborhood Commissions. A **commission** is a group that meets for a special purpose. Each neighborhood commission tells the city council what that community needs. For example, a commission might meet to talk about how to stop crime in a neighborhood.

Reading Check ŏ**Cause and Effect**
What is the effect of having a city council made up of people from all parts of the city?

Summary The Washington, D.C., city government makes laws and provides services for the people in the city. City government leaders include a mayor, the city council, and judges.

❯ **Much of the city government has its offices in the John A. Wilson Building.**

Review

1. **What to Know** How does the city government of Washington, D.C., work?

2. **Vocabulary** How are a **council** and a **commission** different?

3. **Civics and Government** Which branch of city government includes the mayor?

4. **Critical Thinking** Why might citizens in Washington, D.C., think it unfair that they cannot elect a voting member of Congress?

5. **Make a Chart** Make a chart that shows the jobs of the three branches of the city government of Washington, D.C.

6. **Cause and Effect** On a sheet of paper, copy and complete the graphic organizer below.

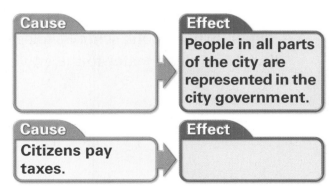

Cause	Effect
	People in all parts of the city are represented in the city government.
Citizens pay taxes.	

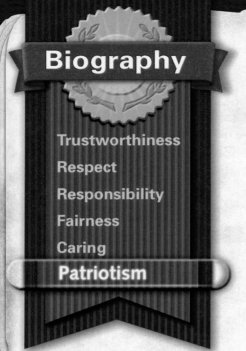

Trustworthiness
Respect
Responsibility
Fairness
Caring
Patriotism

City Leaders

From 1874 until 1975, city leaders in Washington, D.C., were appointed by the President. Since 1975, the people of Washington, D.C., have elected leaders for the city. These leaders have worked hard for the people of the city.

As a young boy, William Winston Seaton became interested in government. In 1812, Seaton moved to Washington, D.C. He and his wife's brother ran a newspaper. They wrote about the activities of Congress. Seaton's writing about government earned people's respect. From 1819 to 1831, Seaton served on the city council. In 1840, he was elected mayor. He served as mayor for ten years. Seaton helped bring public schools, telegraph lines, and clean water to the city.

William Winston Seaton

1785–1866
Character Trait: Patriotism

Walter Washington

1915–2003
Character Trait: Patriotism

Before he was mayor, Walter Washington served for 15 years in the Washington, D.C., municipal government. When there were riots in the city in 1967, Washington wanted to end them peacefully. He said, "I . . . urged angry young people to go home. I asked them to help the people who had been burned out."

In 1975, President Lyndon Johnson appointed Washington mayor of the city. Washington wanted the city to have an elected government. In 1976, he became the city's first elected mayor in recent times.

Sharon Pratt Kelly was born in Washington, D.C. After finishing law school at Howard University, Kelly worked for the power company. She was elected mayor of Washington, D.C., in 1991. She was the first African American woman to be mayor of a major city. She served until 1995.

Sharon Pratt Kelly

1944–
Character Trait: Patriotism

Why Character Counts

1 How did all of these Washington, D.C., leaders show patriotism?

2 What other qualities does a good leader have?

For more resources, go to
www.harcourtschool.com/ss1

A Government of the People

What to Know
How can citizens take part in their government?

Vocabulary
citizen p. 54
responsibility p. 55
committee p. 56
hearing p. 56
jury p. 57

Cause and Effect

Cause	Effect

As a democracy, the United States government gets its power from citizens. **Citizens** are the people who live in and belong to a community. For democracy to work, people need to be active and involved in the government. It is up to the people to make sure their government works well and to protect their freedoms.

> Voting is an important right for citizens.

▶ Adrian Fenty became the mayor of Washington, D.C., in 2007.

Choosing Leaders

One of the most important ways people take part in government is by voting. They elect the leaders who will make decisions for all the people.

Voting is an important right. However, voting is also a responsibility. A **responsibility** is a duty, or something a person must do because it is important.

Running for Office

When people want to get elected, they run for government offices. Whether they step forward to lead as a city council member, the mayor, or a member of Congress, they speak for the people of their community. They try to make the best decisions for the people they represent.

Reading Check ⏱ Cause and Effect
What would happen if citizens did not vote?

Active Citizenship

In the United States, people have the right to say good or bad things about the government. They can give speeches, join marches, or publish their opinions in newspapers. People who do these things want to cause change with their words and actions.

Citizens can even speak out at some government meetings. The Washington, D.C., city council has groups, or **committees**, to study and report on certain city problems. Citizens can join a committee or speak at city council meetings about their concerns.

Sometimes the city holds public hearings. A **hearing** is a special meeting at which city leaders listen to the people. At a hearing, anyone can speak.

D.C. Youth Advisory Council

Young people in Washington, D.C., have a special way to take part in their city government. Young people aged 13 to 22 years can join the D.C. Youth Advisory Council (DCYAC). The DCYAC advises the mayor, city council, and public schools on issues that affect youth. City leaders listen to the suggestions of the DCYAC for making Washington, D.C., a better place for young people.

The DCYAC has 32 members. There are three representatives from each of Washington's eight neighborhood wards, plus eight at-large council members.

Make It Relevant **What kinds of issues do you think affect young people in the city the most?**

➤ **Members of the DCYAC meet with the mayor.**

Serving Justice

People also take part in government by serving on a jury. A **jury** is a group of citizens who attend a trial and then decide whether the person on trial has broken a law. By serving on a jury, people take part in the judicial branch of government.

Reading Check ☼**Cause and Effect**
What can be the effect of speaking out?

Summary Democracy depends on people taking part in government. People do this by voting, by serving on juries, and by exercising their rights. They can also participate in government meetings or hearings or run for office.

❯ Citizens have the responsibility to serve on a jury.

Review

1. **What to Know** How can citizens take part in their government?

2. **Vocabulary** Explain how the **responsibility** of voting comes with the right to vote.

3. **Civics and Government** How can citizens take part in the judicial branch of government?

4. **Critical Thinking** Why are active citizens necessary in a democracy?

5. ✎ **Write a Letter** Write a letter to a person in city government about a problem in your community. Say what you think the city should do about the problem.

6. ⭐(Focus Skill) **Cause and Effect** On a sheet of paper, copy and complete the graphic organizer below.

Cause	Effect
People take part in government.	

Cause	Effect
People vote.	

Identify Multiple Causes and Effects

Why It Matters Understanding the causes and effects of an action can help you understand problems in your community. It can help people make choices when they take part in government.

❯ Learn

Use these steps to identify multiple causes and effects.

Step 1 Look for the effects. Decide whether there is more than one effect.

Step 2 Look for the causes of the effects.

Step 3 Think about how the causes and effects are related.

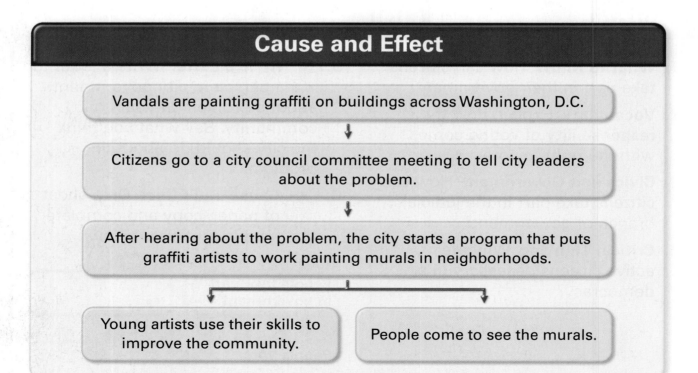

Cause and Effect

Vandals are painting graffiti on buildings across Washington, D.C.

↓

Citizens go to a city council committee meeting to tell city leaders about the problem.

↓

After hearing about the problem, the city starts a program that puts graffiti artists to work painting murals in neighborhoods.

Young artists use their skills to improve the community.

People come to see the murals.

❯ Practice

You have seen more and more graffiti around the city lately. You want to do to something to help get rid of it. What would be the causes and effects of your actions? Use the diagram to answer these questions.

1 What is the first cause shown on the diagram? What is the effect of that cause?

2 Which event had more than one effect?

3 Identify one event that is both a cause and an effect.

❯ Apply

Make It Relevant Think of another kind of problem in your neighborhood or school. Make a chart like the one shown here to show several causes and effects of taking action on the problem.

Visual Summary

Governments keep order and help people meet their needs.

— Summarize the Unit —

 Cause and Effect Complete the graphic organizer to show that you understand the important causes and effects of government.

Cause
People create governments.

Effect

Cause
People take part in government.

Effect

TEST PREP ✓ Vocabulary

Identify the term from the word bank that correctly matches each definition.

1. a representative to another country

2. a duty

3. having to do with a city

4. a group of citizens who attend a trial and then decide whether the person on trial has broken a law

5. national

6. a group that meets to make laws

7. a group that studies and reports on certain city problems

Word Bank

federal p. 40

ambassador p. 44

municipal p. 48

council p. 49

responsibility p. 55

committee p. 56

jury p. 57

 Washington, D.C., has a municipal government that makes laws for the city.

 People can take part in and influence the government.

Facts and Main Ideas

Answer these questions

8. What is the main job of government?

9. What kind of problems and issues does each level of government handle?

10. What are three ways to take part in government?

Write the letter of the best choice.

11. Which is the part of government that carries out the laws?
    A the legislative branch
    B the executive branch
    C the judicial branch
    D a committee

12. What group or person makes the laws in Washington, D.C.?
    A the mayor
    B the city council
    C the Advisory Neighborhood Commissions
    D the courts

Critical Thinking

13. Why are rules necessary in a community?

14. Why do you think it was decided that the nation's capital should not belong to any one state?

Skills

Identify Multiple Causes and Effects

15. Look at the diagram on page 58. What is the effect of citizens going to the city council committee meeting?

writing

Write a Brochure Write a brochure that encourages people to take part in their local government.

Write a Letter Write a letter to the D.C. Youth Advisory Council. Say why you would be a good council member and what problems you want to help solve.

Fun with Social Studies

Government Tic-Tac-Toe

Find three things in a row that are related to local government.

Tic-Tac-Toe

What's the Word?

Fill in the missing letters. Find the number in the words and write its letter on the lines below to answer the riddle.

1 A group of people chosen to study problems.
c o ☐ m ☐ ☐ t e ☐
     8   1

2 A special meeting where city leaders listen to the people.
☐ ☐ ☐ r ☐ ☐ g
5 3

3 A representative of a country sent to another country.
☐ ☐ b ☐ s ☐ ☐ d ☐ ☐
6   9

4 A city or local government.
m u ☐ ☐ c ☐ ☐ a ☐
      4   2

5 A group of people who meet to make laws.
☐ o u ☐ ☐ ☐ l
   7

What are the largest ants in the world?
e ☐ ☐ ☐ ☐ ☐ a ☐ ☐ ☐
1 2 3 4 5 6 7 8 9

The Economy of Washington, D.C.

The Big Idea

Meeting Needs

People depend on one another to produce, buy, and sell goods and services.

What to Know

- ✓ How is the way people meet their needs now different from the way they met their needs in the past?

- ✓ How does Washington, D.C., meet the economic needs of its citizens?

- ✓ How do communities pay for services for citizens?

Vocabulary

barter   To trade without using money.
(page 70)

plantation   A large farm. (page 73)

transportation Ways to move from one place to another. (page 78)

good An item that can be bought or sold. (page 68)

recreation Any activity that people do for fun. (page 78)

GO ONLINE For more resources, go to www.harcourtschool.com/ss1

Lesson 1

Meeting Needs

What to Know
Over time, how have people changed their ways of meeting needs?

Vocabulary
need p. 66
good p. 68
service p. 68
specialize p. 69
barter p. 70

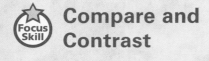

Compare and Contrast

People live in Washington, D.C., because the city provides much of what they need. **Needs** are the things that people must have to live. People need water, food, clothing, and shelter.

Think about what Washington, D.C., was before it was a city. How did people meet their needs then? How do you think meeting needs then was different from the way people meet their needs today?

Using Resources

Long ago, Native Americans used the natural resources around them to meet their needs. They gathered berries and acorns, hunted animals, and trapped fish. From the plants and animals, they made clothing and tools.

In time, people grew their food. Native Americans grew corn, beans, and squash. Today, people still use the land to grow food. Most of the food that people in the Washington, D.C., area eat is grown on large farms all across the country.

Reading Check ☼**Compare and Contrast**
How is the way Native Americans used the land similar to the way people today use the land?

66 ▪ **Unit 3**

HUNTING AND GATHERING The earliest people met their basic needs by hunting animals and gathering plants.

SIMPLE FARMING Then people began to grow their food.

SPECIALIZING In time, workers specialized in making one kind of product.

MANUFACTURING Later, workers in factories used machines to make products.

Illustration How do you think farming changed the way people lived long ago?

Providing Goods and Services

Today, people can buy much of what they need from businesses. Some businesses make or sell goods. **Goods** are things that can be bought or sold. Other businesses provide services. **Services** are the kinds of work that people do for others for money. School bus drivers, doctors, servers in restaurants, and automobile mechanics are some workers who provide services.

Goods Start with Resources

People use natural resources to make goods. Early settlers made furniture from the trees in the forests. From iron, they made plows and other tools. They used the power of moving water to turn large stones. Those stones ground wheat and corn into flour.

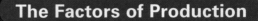

The Factors of Production

Illustration Businesses use three kind of resources to produce goods or services. Why do you think the factory was built near a river?

Natural resources
Natural resources are resources found in nature that people can use. They include trees and water.

Capital resources
Businesses also need capital resources, such as tools and machines, to get the work done. A factory is a kind of capital resource, too.

Human resources
Businesses also need human resources, or people, to do the work.

▶ A store that sells pet supplies is an example of a specialized business.

In time, people used machines to manufacture, or make, goods more easily out of these natural resources. For example, in textile mills, machines wove wool into cloth. The machines did the work in much less time than it took to weave cloth by hand.

Specializing

Many different businesses specialize. To **specialize** is to make or sell one kind of product or service. In the past, there were shipbuilders and blacksmiths around Washington, D.C. Today, specialized businesses in Washington, D.C., might include a store that sells bicycles or a company that designs websites.

Reading Check ◉ **Compare and Contrast**
What is the difference between goods and services?

The $1 Bill

Background The United States government prints about 37 million bills each day. About half of them are $1 bills.

Every bill has a serial number so that the government can keep track of the money that is printed.

The seal of the Department of the Treasury

DBQ Document-Based Question Why do you think the $1 bill has a portrait of George Washington on it?

Different Kinds of Money

To get goods, people need to trade. In the past, people often traded by bartering. To **barter** is to trade without using money. Native Americans traveled to other villages to barter. They exchanged tobacco and corn for goods they did not have, such as seashells and copper.

Later, European settlers traded with Native Americans. In exchange for food, the settlers gave them metal tools made in Europe.

Bartering still happens today. For example, a painter might paint a plumber's house if the plumber will fix the painter's leaky pipes. Have you ever traded with a friend? That is bartering, too.

Using Money to Trade

Today, people most often trade money for goods and services. Money makes trading easier. Coins and bills are small and light to carry. Also, everyone knows how much they are worth.

▶ Most goods can be paid for with money.

Reading Check **Generalize**
How does money make trading easier?

Summary As in the past, people use resources to get what they need. In the past, people got what they need from the world around them. Often, they traded to get what they needed. Today, people use money to buy things that they need.

Review

1. **What to Know** How has the way people meet their needs changed over time?

2. **Vocabulary** Write a description of a business that **specializes**.

3. **Economics** What are some ways people pay for goods and services?

4. **Critical Thinking Make It Relevant** What are some goods and services you could use to barter?

5. **Make a Chart** Make a chart with two columns. In the first column, list three natural resources. In the second column, list how people use each natural resource.

6. **Compare and Contrast**
(Focus Skill) On a sheet of paper, copy and complete the graphic organizer below.

Topic 1
Water
Similar
Topic 2
Shelter

Businesses Change

What to Know
How have businesses and jobs in Washington, D.C., changed over time?

Vocabulary

plantation p. 73

manufacturing p. 74
tourism p. 75

Compare and Contrast

Topic 1

Similar

Topic 2

The year is 1891. You are standing on Pennsylvania Avenue at 7th Street. You have come to shop at Center Market, the city's biggest marketplace. Outside the market, people are selling meats, fish, cheese, eggs, and many other delicious foods. Inside, there are many more good things to buy.

▶ George Washington owned a plantation called Mount Vernon near Washington, D.C.

Early Businesses

Washington, D.C., was built to be the center of government for our country. From the very beginning, most people came to the city to help run the government. In addition to elected leaders, people who worked for the government included lawyers, scientists, printers, librarians, and clerks.

Carpenters, bricklayers, and other workers also moved to the city. They helped build government buildings such as the United States Capitol and the White House. They also built homes and businesses.

Farming

People in the city could not always make everything that they needed themselves. They depended on other workers outside the city. Long ago, the area around Washington, D.C., was used mostly for farming. In the 1700s and 1800s, large farms called **plantations** grew crops such as tobacco.

Factories

Starting in the 1700s and 1800s, more businesses began to make products by using machines. This way of making products is called **manufacturing**. Factories, lumberyards, and flour mills opened in and around Washington, D.C. In the late 1800s, the J.E. Hanger factory made a unique product. It built artificial, or human-made, legs for soldiers wounded in war. Workers at the Schmid factory on 12th Street made paper boxes.

Some factories were built near the Potomac River, the Anacostia River, and the C&O Canal. Raw materials, such as wood, could be carried on ships to the factories. Then finished goods could be shipped on the waterways from the factories to markets.

Reading Check ☼ **Compare and Contrast**
For what was the land around Washington, D.C., first used?

> **A factory on Greenleaf's Point in the mid-1800s**

Businesses Today

Today, more Washingtonians work for the government than in any other industry. Tourism is also one of the top industries in Washington, D.C. **Tourism** is the selling of goods and services to tourists. Hotels and restaurants are part of the tourism industry.

Reading Check ☼**Compare and Contrast**
What kinds of jobs do most people in Washington, D.C., have today?

Summary The economy of Washington, D.C., has always been centered around the government. Farming and manufacturing were important in the past. Today, tourism is one of the city's top industries.

❯ About one in four workers in Washington, D.C., work for the federal government. This woman works for the Bureau of Engraving and Printing.

Review

1. **What to Know** How are the businesses and jobs in Washington, D.C., different today from what they were in the past?

2. **Vocabulary** Use the term **tourism** in a sentence to explain its meaning.

3. **Geography** Where were some factories built in Washington, D.C.? Why?

4. **Critical Thinking** Why do economies change over time?

5. **Make a Poster** Make a poster that shows the economy of Washington, D.C., in the past and the city's economy today.

6. **Compare and Contrast** On a sheet of paper, copy and complete the graphic organizer below.

Topic 1

Similar
are important
industries

Topic 2

Lesson  3

Providing Services

What to Know
How does Washington, D.C., meet the needs of its citizens?

Vocabulary
transportation p. 78
recreation p. 78
tax p. 79

Compare and Contrast
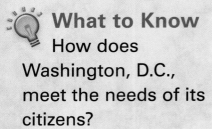

You are at home, looking out the window. The city bus pulls up. Passengers hurry on and off. One of them is your neighbor. She is carrying a stack of books. She must be returning from the public library, you think. Your mother then tells you to take out the garbage. Tomorrow, the city will pick up the trash in your neighborhood.

❯ Washington, D.C., provides different kinds of services to the people who live there.

Trash removal

Public transportation

76

Public Works and Health and Safety

Part of the job of the government of Washington, D.C., is to provide services to meet the daily needs of residents. The city repairs streets, collects trash, and makes sure that the community has clean water. In the winter, the city removes snow from the streets.

The fire department of Washington, D.C., puts out fires and rescues people who are hurt. The police department makes sure traffic laws and other laws are obeyed.

Some cities provide clinics and hospitals. People in Washington, D.C., who cannot pay for health care can go to the doctors at the Washington Free Clinic.

Reading Check **Generalize**
How does Washington, D.C., make sure its residents are safe and healthy?

Public libraries

Fire and police protection

> Tax money was used to help pay for a new baseball stadium in Washington, D.C.

Other Services

The city runs public libraries and schools for its residents. Poor families can get help from the city to pay for housing. The city also helps some people find jobs.

People in the city need **transportation**, or ways to move from one place to another. Washington, D.C., has a system of public buses, subways, and trains. They run throughout the city and in nearby Virginia and Maryland.

Some cities also provide places for recreation (reh•kree•AY•shuhn). **Recreation** is any activity that people do for fun. These places include parks, pools, and sports fields. At Rock Creek Park, people like to hike, jog, rollerblade, and have picnics.

Reading Check ŏCompare and Contrast
In what way are all the city's services alike?

Taxes

The services that the city provides cost money. People pay for government services when they pay taxes. A **tax** is money that citizens pay to the government. All citizens must pay their taxes.

There are three main kinds of taxes. People pay sales tax when they buy goods at stores. People who own homes or land pay property tax. A third kind of tax is income tax. People pay income tax based on how much money they make each year.

Reading Check ŏCompare and Contrast
What are the different kinds of taxes?

Summary Washington, D.C., provides important services for its residents. They include transportation, police and fire protection, health care, and recreation. Many city services are paid for with tax money.

Molly's Pet Store

Order Number 14432

At Molly's, Service Is Number One

Fish Tank	22.49
Goldfish	1.49
Gravel	2.49
Fish Food	1.99
4 Items Subtotal	28.46
Sales Tax 5.75%	1.64
Total	30.10
Cash Payment	31.00
Change	.90

Save all receipts
THANK YOU

▶ People in Washington, D.C., pay a 5.75 percent sales tax when they buy goods at stores.

Review

1. **What to Know** What are some ways in which Washington, D.C., meets the economic needs of its citizens?

2. **Vocabulary** Use the terms **transportation** and **recreation** to describe services the city provides for its residents.

3. **Economics** How does Washington, D.C., pay for the services it provides for citizens?

4. **Critical Thinking** Do you think people see taxes as a good or bad part of our society? Explain.

5. ✏️ **Write a Paragraph** Write a paragraph describing the three main kinds of taxes. Why do we pay them?

6. ⭐(Focus Skill) **Compare and Contrast** On a sheet of paper, copy and complete the graphic organizer below.

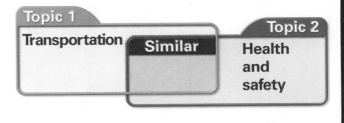

Topic 1
Transportation

Similar

Topic 2
Health and safety

The Metro

Background In 1967, Washington, D.C., and seven nearby cities and counties in Maryland and Virginia formed the Washington Metropolitan Area Transit Authority (WMATA) to build and run a subway and bus system. Today, this system is known as the Metro.

DBQ **Document-Based Question** Study these primary sources and answer the questions.

FARECARD

Farecards can be bought from vending machines. Passengers insert their farecards through the fare gate at the beginning and end of their trip.

DBQ **1** What is the value of this farecard?

$10.00

270844

THE FUTURE IS RIDING ON METRO

INSERT

See important message on back.

FARECARD VALUE

TRADE IN

©WMATA

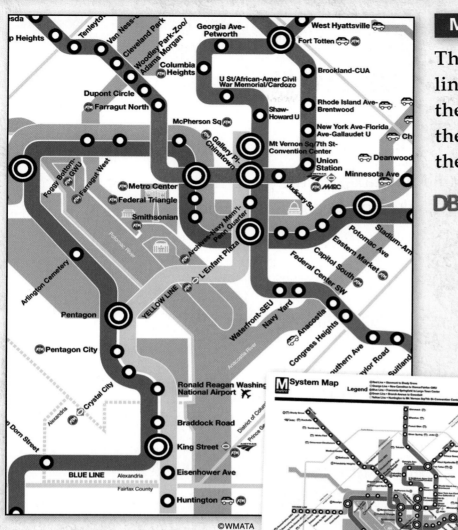
©WMATA

METRO SYSTEM MAP

The Metro has five subway lines: the Orange Line, the Blue Line, the Red Line, the Yellow Line, and the Green Line.

DBQ ❸ Which line would you take to go from Arlington National Cemetery to the Smithsonian Institution?

DBQ ❹ Which line has stops at the Navy Yard, Mt. Vernon Square, and U Street?

POCKET GUIDE

The Pocket Guide to the Metro system lists the points of interest that are near each Metro station.

DBQ ❷ At which Metro station would you get off to see the U.S. Botanic Gardens?

©WMATA

GARDENS & PARKS
<u>U. S. Botanic Gardens</u>   *1st St. & Independence Ave. SW*
Federal Center SW ■ ■ 32, 34, 35, 36, P6
<u>Dumbarton Oaks</u>   *1703 32nd St. NW, Georgetown*
Foggy Bottom-GWU ■ ■, Rosslyn ■ ■, Dupont Circle ■ with transfer to
Georgetown Shuttle, 32, 34, 35, 36, D2, D6
<u>Kenilworth Aquatic Gardens</u>   *Douglas & Anacostia Sts. NE*
Deanwood ■ V7, V8
<u>National Arboretum</u>   *3501 New York Ave. NE*
B2, X6
<u>   ...ological Park</u>   *3001 Connecticut Ave. NW*

WRITE ABOUT IT

Describe the route to take to get from the station closest to where you live to Reagan National Airport.

GO ONLINE For more resources, go to www.harcourtschool.com/ss1

Make Economic Choices

Why It Matters People pay taxes to the government. The government must make good economic choices when spending the taxes.

❱ Learn

The government follows these steps when deciding how to spend taxes.

Step 1 What is the **trade-off**? When the government chooses to pay for one service, it is giving up the chance to pay for a different one.

Step 1 What is the **opportunity cost**? This is what the government must give up to get what it wants.

❱ One way Washington, D.C., meets the recreational needs of its citizens is by building bicycle paths in the city.

❯ The city could also spend part of its budget to put a water fountain in a park. How do you think this would benefit the community?

❯ Practice

The city has $3,000 in tax money to improve the park. They could put in a water fountain. It would cost $2,000. Or they could fix the potholes in the bicycle path, which would also cost $2,000.

1. What is the trade-off if the city chooses the water fountain? What is the trade-off if the city fixes the bike path?

2. What is the opportunity cost for each?

3. What do you think the city should do? Why?

❯ Apply

Make It Relevant What are two things in your community that your local government could spend tax money on? What are the trade-offs and opportunity costs for each?

Citizenship Skills

Visual Summary

People buy goods and services to meet their needs.

— **Summarize the Unit** —

Compare and Contrast Complete the graphic organizer to compare and contrast economies.

Topic 1

Washington, D.C.'s Economy in the Past

Similar

Topic 2

Washington, D.C.'s Economy Today

 **Vocabulary**

Write the correct term from the word bank to complete each sentence.

1. The grocery store sells many _____, including milk and bananas.

2. The barber shop offers _____ such as haircuts and trims.

3. The store _____ in selling only hats.

4. The city government raised the _____ to help pay for a new school.

5. The students need _____ to get to the soccer game.

Word Bank

specialize p. 69   **tax** p. 79

services p. 67   **transportation** p. 79

goods p. 67

Today, the economy of Washington, D.C., is based on the government and tourism.

Washington, D.C., meets the economic needs of its citizens.

 ## Facts and Main Ideas

Answer these questions.

6. How have the ways people meet their needs changed over time?

7. What is the main part of the economy of Washington, D.C., today?

8. Why does the government collect taxes?

Write the letter of the best choice.

9. How did Native Americans long ago meet their needs?
   A They raised crops to sell for money.
   B They hunted and gathered, farmed, and bartered.
   C They went to the grocery store and the mall.
   D They went to Europe to trade.

10. What service in Washington, D.C., is paid for with taxes?
    A movie theaters
    B restaurants
    C taxis
    D police protection

 ## Critical Thinking

11. Why must everyone pay taxes?

12. **Make It Relevant** What would our lives be like if there were no taxes?

 ## Skills

Make Economic Choices

13. Imagine that you have $30. You want to buy a new video game for $20 and a new DVD for $15. What would you choose? What is the trade-off? What is the opportunity cost?

writing

Write a Paragraph Write a short paragraph describing a kind of business that is needed in your community.

Write a Speech Write a speech about why public transportation is a good service to have in Washington, D.C.

Fun with Social Studies

1 "I drive around Washington, D.C., for my job. People get on and off my vehicle at stops. Taxes help pay for my salary."

2 "I get to work in a city park every day. I take care of the trees and plant new flowers. I also cut the grass. I'm proud that I can help make Washington, D.C., look beautiful."

3 "I work in the tourism industry. I check people into their hotel rooms when they come to visit the city. I also answer any questions about the city they might have."

4 "I work in a city hospital. It is my job to make sure that the people of Washington, D.C., stay healthy."

What's My Job?

Match the jobs in the word bank to the correct description below.

hotel clerk, bus driver, doctor, gardener

Under Construction

abc VOCABULARY

Finish building the terms on the left by adding the word blocks on the right.

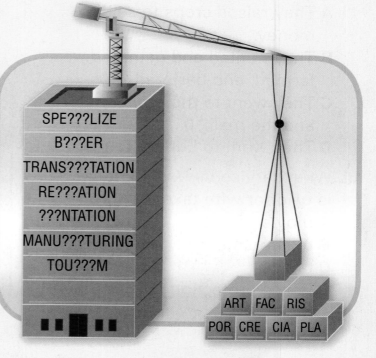

SPE???LIZE
B???ER
TRANS???TATION
RE???ATION
???NTATION
MANU???TURING
TOU???M

ART FAC RIS
POR CRE CIA PLA

The History of Washington, D.C.

The Big Idea

History

People and events in history have shaped the character of Washington, D.C.

What to Know

✓ What are key events in the history of Washington, D.C?

✓ How has Washington, D.C., changed over time?

✓ In what ways has Washington, D.C., become a unique capital city and a multicultural urban center?

longhouse   A long and narrow Native American shelter. (page 90)

amendment   A change to the Constitution. (page 107)

colony A place ruled by another country. (page 92)

civil war A war in which people of the same country fight each other. (page 98)

nomad A person who moved from place to place hunting and gathering. (page 91)

GO ONLINE For more resources, go to www.harcourtschool.com/ss1

Lesson 1 People Long Ago

What to Know
Who were the first people to live in what is now Washington, D.C.?

Vocabulary
longhouse p. 90
nomad p. 91
colony p. 92

Focus Skill Generalize

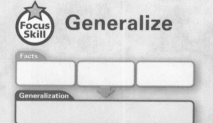

Facts

Generalization

You climb aboard a time machine that takes you back to the year 1600. Where your classroom was is now a forest. You walk through the forest to a river. There you see a circle of shelters surrounded by a tall fence made of poles. The buildings are long and narrow and have curved roofs. They are called **longhouses**. You realize that you are looking at an early Native American village.

▶ Algonquian villages usually had from 10 to 30 longhouses.

> This cape may have been worn by an Algonquian chief. It is decorated with shells.

The Earliest People

About 12,000 years ago, Native American groups arrived in what is now Washington, D.C. The earliest people were **nomads**. They moved from place to place hunting and gathering. Over time, they settled in permanent, or lasting, villages.

The Piscataway

The Piscataway (pih•SCAT•uh•way) were among the Native American groups who lived in the area. They were among the people to speak an Algonquian (al•GAHN•kwee•uhn) language. Algonquian speakers lived in similar kinds of villages and used the region's natural resources in similar ways.

The Potomac River was important to the Piscataway. It gave them fish to eat and water to drink. The people also used the river to water their crops.

The Piscataway traveled on the river to trade with other Native American groups. A trading village called Nacotchtanck (NAH•kahtch•tuhnk) grew near the mouth of the Anacostia River.

> An Algonquian warrior

Reading Check ᔅGeneralize
How was the Potomac River important to the Piscataway?

Europeans Arrive

In the 1600s, explorers from Europe arrived. They hoped to find treasure in North America and to spread their religion. Others came to claim land. Captain John Smith of England was one of the first Europeans to explore the Potomac River. He and his crew wrote about the people they met and the land. The amount of fish in the river surprised them. "We attempted to catch [the fish] with a frying pan," Smith wrote, "but we found it a bad instrument to catch fish with."

English Colonies

In 1634, a group of settlers from England arrived in the area. They came to start a colony. A **colony** is a place ruled by another country.

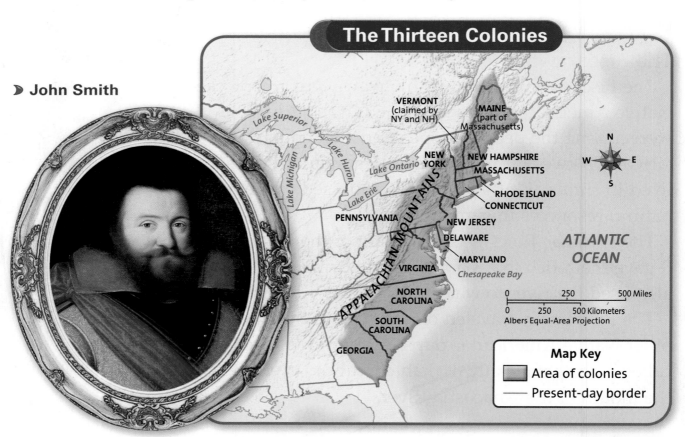

▶ **John Smith**

The Thirteen Colonies

VERMONT
(claimed by
NY and NH)

MAINE
(part of
Massachusetts)

Lake Superior

Lake Michigan

Lake Huron

Lake Ontario

NEW
YORK

NEW HAMPSHIRE

MASSACHUSETTS

Lake Erie

RHODE ISLAND
CONNECTICUT

PENNSYLVANIA

NEW JERSEY

DELAWARE

APPALACHIAN MOUNTAINS

MARYLAND

VIRGINIA

Chesapeake Bay

NORTH
CAROLINA

SOUTH
CAROLINA

GEORGIA

ATLANTIC
OCEAN

N
W   E
S

0   250   500 Miles
0   250   500 Kilometers
Albers Equal-Area Projection

Map Key
Area of colonies
— Present-day border

MAP SKILL **Regions** This map shows the English colonies in North America. What colonies were nearest to where Washington, D.C., is now?

At first, the Piscataway lived peacefully with the colonists. But problems soon arose. The colonists took away the Piscataway's best land. They also unknowingly brought diseases that made the Piscataway sick. Many Piscataway died, and some moved west.

Reading Check ☼**Generalize**
Why did John Smith explore the Potomac River?

Summary Native Americans have been living in the area that became Washington, D.C., for thousands of years. One group was the Piscataway. In the 1600s, people from Europe settled on the land.

➤ **Jamestown, in Virginia, was the first permanent English settlement in North America.**

Review

1. **What to Know** Who were the first people to live in what is now Washington, D.C.?

2. **Vocabulary** Write a description of a **colony**.

3. **History** Why was there conflict between the European settlers and the Native Americans?

4. **Critical Thinking** Why did the Piscataway choose to live in the area that is now Washington, D.C.?

5. ✏ **Write a Journal Entry** Imagine that you are traveling with Captain John Smith up the Potomac River. Write a journal entry describing what you see.

6. (Focus Skill) **Generalize** On a sheet of paper, copy and complete the graphic organizer below.

Facts

⬇

Generalization
The life of the Piscataway centered around the Potomac River.

Lesson 2

Shaping Washington, D.C.

What to Know
What events shaped Washington, D.C., in the 1700s, 1800s, and 1900s?

Vocabulary
independence p. 95
survey p. 96
civil war p. 98

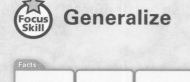

Generalize

Facts		

Generalization

General George Washington has brought a group of people to a spot of land overlooking the Potomac River. He points at the swampy land in the distance. "One day soon," he tells the group, "a great capital city will rise on that land."

❯ Selecting the site of the capital city

▶ United States leaders met to write a plan of government for the new nation.

Making a New Nation

By the 1700s, Britain had 13 colonies in North America. In time, people in the colonies wanted to be free from Britain. The colonists fought a war with Britain. It was called the American Revolution. They finally won their **independence**, or freedom, in 1783. The colonies became the United States of America. George Washington was the first President of the United States.

The new country needed a capital city. Some people wanted the capital to be in the North. Others wanted it to be in the South.

Finally, Congress made a decision. Virginia and Maryland would each give up some of its land on the Potomac River. At the time, this spot was at the center of the country. The city would be called Washington in honor of the President.

⚡Fast Fact

Before Washington, D.C., was built, Philadelphia and New York City each served as capital of the United States.

Reading Check ☼Generalize
How was Washington, D.C., selected and named as the capital city?

Benjamin Banneker

Black Heritage USA 15c

Washington in the 1700s

It was up to President Washington to decide on the exact site for the capital city. In 1791, he chose land on the east bank of the Potomac River near the mouth of the Anacostia River, not far from his home in Mount Vernon.

Planning the Capital

The land chosen by Washington was covered with woods and swamps. It was going to take a lot of work to turn this wilderness into a grand city.

One of the first jobs was to **survey**, or mark, the boundaries of the city. Washington asked Andrew Ellicott and Benjamin Banneker to do this.

❭ Benjamin Banneker and Andrew Ellicott

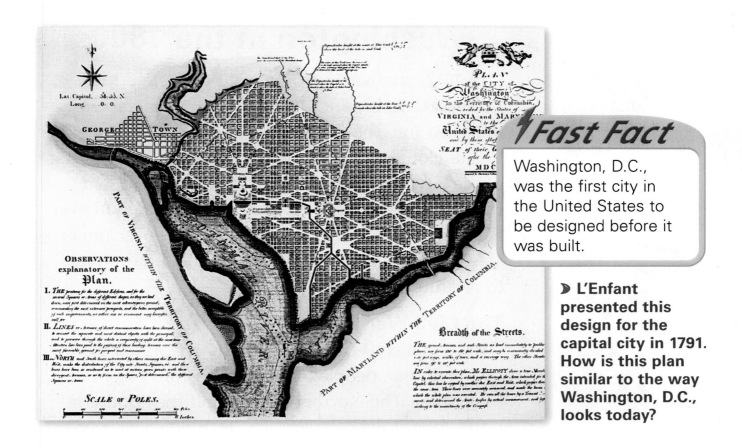

Fast Fact

Washington, D.C., was the first city in the United States to be designed before it was built.

▶ **L'Enfant presented this design for the capital city in 1791. How is this plan similar to the way Washington, D.C., looks today?**

The area that Ellicott and Banneker marked out was shaped like a diamond. Each side of the diamond was 10 miles long.

Washington hired a French artist named Pierre L'Enfant (lahn•FAHN) to plan the city. L'Enfant designed a city with wide streets that reached out, like the spokes in a wheel, from two main centers. In one center was the Capitol. This building is where Congress meets. In the other center was the President's house. L'Enfant also planned parks at nearly every major corner and many places for monuments. In 1800, the federal government moved to the city.

Reading Check 🔆**Generalize**
Why are the Capitol and the President's house focal points of L'Enfant's design for the capital city?

Washington in the 1800s

Fast Fact

As she fled the White House during the War of 1812, First Lady Dolley Madison saved a famous portrait of George Washington from being destroyed.

In 1812, another war between Britain and the United States began. In 1814, British soldiers marched into the capital city. They set fire to the White House, the Capitol building, and other parts of the city. One Washingtonian of that time said that it was "not expected that Washington will ever again be the seat of government." The government stayed in Washington, D.C., but it took many years to rebuild the city.

The Civil War

In 1861, a civil war broke out in the United States. In a **civil war**, people of the same country fight each other. The Northern states and the Southern states fought over slavery. The terrible war lasted until 1865.

❯ **This mural shows the British attack on Washington, D.C., in 1814.**

1814

▶ **African Americans in Washington, D.C., celebrate the end of slavery in the capital in 1862.**

In 1862, Congress passed a law that ended slavery in Washington, D.C. Thousands of freed African Americans moved to the capital city. "We came . . . not just for work," said one woman, "but for a real better life."

Changes for the Better

The number of people living in Washington grew quickly during the Civil War and afterwards. The city could not meet the needs of all the new people. People could not find housing. The city did not have a sewer system. Garbage was dumped in creeks and canals.

Starting in 1871, leaders worked to improve the city. Workers paved streets and built a sewer system. They cleaned up canals and planted trees. In 1877, telephones were installed. In the early 1880s, the city got electric lights.

Reading Check 🔥**Generalize**
What events shaped the nation's capital in the 1800s?

D.C. in the 1900s

In 1900, Washington, D.C., celebrated its one-hundredth birthday as the capital of the United States. The capital was now a city of close to 300,000 people. The 1900s brought much more growth.

The United States fought in two world wars in the first part of the twentieth century. Hundreds of thousands of people came to work in the capital to help in the war effort.

In the 1930s, the country faced hard times. Many people were out of work. The government hired people to build roads, bridges, and parks. In Washington, D.C., they built the Jefferson Memorial, the Supreme Court Building, and the National Gallery of Art, as well as other important buildings and monuments, during this time.

❱ **The Supreme Court Building was built from 1932 to 1935.**

Home Rule

For much of the history of Washington, D.C., city leaders were appointed by Congress. For many years, people in the city wanted to have more political rights. In 1961, residents of the District were first allowed to vote for President. Then in 1974, the city held its first elections. The people elected Walter Washington as the first mayor of Washington, D.C.

Reading Check **ŎGeneralize**
How did the city change in the 1900s?

Summary Washington, D.C., was built in the late 1700s to be the capital of the United States. The city changed and grew during the 1700s, 1800s, and 1900s.

❯ **Walter Washington being sworn into office, 1975**

Review

1. **What to Know** What events shaped Washington, D.C., in the 1700s, 1800s, and 1900s?

2. **Vocabulary** Write a sentence about **independence**.

3. **History** Why did African Americans move to Washington, D.C., in the 1800s?

4. **Critical Thinking** How did the Civil War change Washington, D.C.?

5. **Create a Brochure** Create a brochure that shows the accomplishments of an important figure in the history of Washington, D.C.

6. **Generalize** On a sheet of paper, copy and complete the graphic organizer below.

Facts
Wars, government acts, and other major events affected the growth of Washington, D.C.

Generalization
The life of the Piscataway centered around the Potomac River.

The United States Capitol

Background The United States government held a contest in 1792 for the design of a new Capitol building. The prize was $500 and a piece of land in the city. A design by Dr. William Thornton was named the winning plan on Aril 5, 1793.

DBQ **Document-Based Question** Study these primary sources and answer the questions.

NEWSPAPER NOTICE

A newspaper notice on March 14, 1792, announced the contest to design a new Capitol building.

DBQ **1** According to the notice, what features were to be part of the Capitol?

Ware, remarkably Cheap for

s to Rent, on Leafe, or Sell, which he lives, as may be Applicants HAIR-POWDER, of the up for Exportation, or home Feb. 28. w&f...

ealy, Silver-plater, ..LY acquaints his friends and general, that he has removed to No 147, Chefnut ftreet, nd Fifth ftreets, where he E, with ftrong fheet filver, moft improved manner, every ch of bufinefs; and will war- e equal to any imported from will furnifh complete fets of a cheaper rate than any other ; and has now for fale an ele- ir f horfes. w&f2w

ed, and for Sale by IIN MASON, of Market ftreet Wharf, pply of Frefh lover Seed, l beft Britifh E TWINE; n Affortment of I L S. d4w n Clark.

an eftimate of the cubic feet of brick work com- pofing the whole mafs of the walls. *The Commiffioners.*

March 14, 1792.

{ WASHINGTON, }
{ In the Territory of Columbia. }

A PREMIUM,

OF a lot in this city, to be defignated by im- partial judges, and 500 dollars; or a medal of that value, at the option of the party, will be given by the Commiffioners of the Federal Buil- dings, to the perfon, who, before the 15th day of July, 1792, fhall produce to them, the moft approved plan, if adopted by them, for a Capi- tol to be erected in this City, and 250 dollars, or a medal, for the plan deemed next in merit to the one they fhall adopt. The building to be of brick, and to contain the following apart- ments, to wit:

A conference room; } Sufficient to ac-
A room for the Re- } commodate 300
prefentatives; } perfons each.
A lobby, or antichamber to the latter;
A Senate room of 1200 fquare feet area;
An antichamber, or lobby to the laft;
⎫ Thefe rooms to be of full elevation

12 rooms of 600 fquare feet area, each, for committee rooms and clerk's offices, to be of half the elevation of the former. Drawings will be expected of the ground plats, elevations of each front, and fections through the building in fuch directions as may be necefary to explain the internal ftructure; and an eftimate of the cubic feet of brick-work compofing the whole mafs of the walls.
The Commiffioners.

March 14, 1792.

Juft Publifhed,
BY THOMAS DOBSON,
Bookfeller, at the *Stone-Houfe*, in Second-ftreet, Philadelphia,
VOLUME V.
OF
ENCYCLOPEDIA

REJECTED PLANS

Plans by Charles Wintersmith and James Diamond were among 17 plans that did not win.

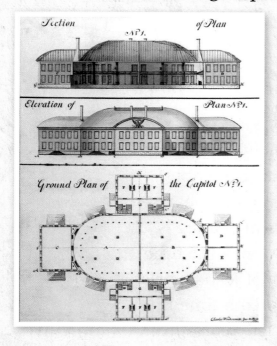

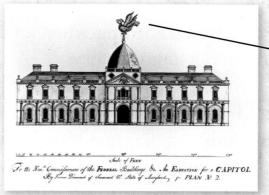

James Diamond's plan featured a giant eagle on top of a dome.

DBQ ❷ Why do you think James Diamond thought an eagle would be a good symbol to put on the Capitol?

THORNTON'S WINNING ENTRY

The building designed by Dr. William Thornton had three sections.

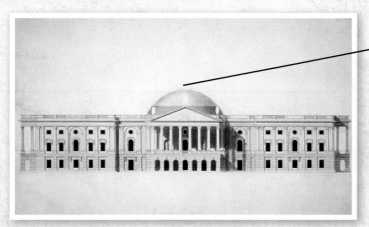

The central section was topped by a low dome. On each side of this section were wings for the Senate and the House of Representatives.

DBQ ❸ In Thornton's plan, the wings for the Senate and the House of Representatives are of equal size. Why do you think such a plan was chosen?

WRITE ABOUT IT

Write a paragraph about why you think United States leaders wanted the public to design the Capitol building.

GO ONLINE For more resources, go to www.harcourtschool.com/ss1

Read a Time Line

Why It Matters Learning when an event took place helps you understand history.

❯ Learn

A **time line** is a diagram that shows when and in what order events took place. Time lines can show events that took place during one month, one year, ten years, hundreds of years, or thousands of years.

You may see the letters *B.C.* and *A.D.* on some time lines. Many people today use the birth of Jesus Christ to date events. Events on the *B.C.* side of the time line took place *before* the birth of Jesus Christ. Years *after* the birth of Christ are labeled *A.D.* Some time lines use *B.C.E.*, or "before the Common Era," to replace *B.C.* and *C.E.*, or "Common Era," to replace *A.D.*

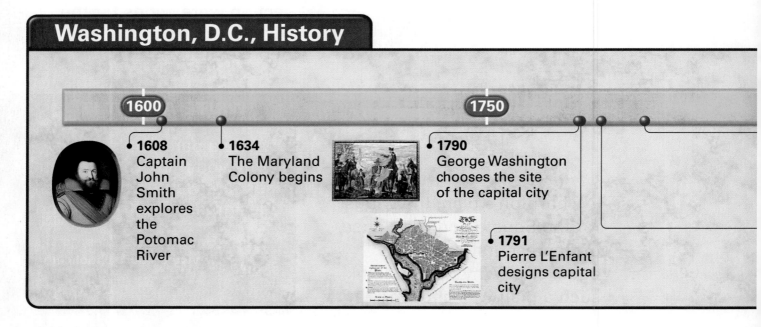

Washington, D.C., History

1600   1750

1608 Captain John Smith explores the Potomac River

1634 The Maryland Colony begins

1790 George Washington chooses the site of the capital city

1791 Pierre L'Enfant designs capital city

You may also notice *c.* beside a date on a time line. It stands for *circa*, which means "approximately," or "about." Time lines use *c.* when the exact date is not known.

▶ Practice

Use the time line to answer these questions.

1 Did John Smith explore the Potomac River before or after the Maryland Colony was founded?

2 How long after George Washington selected the site for the capital city did the federal government move to Washington, D.C.?

3 Which was finished first, the Lincoln Memorial or the the United States Capitol?

▶ Apply

Make It Relevant Make a time line showing important events in the history of your community.

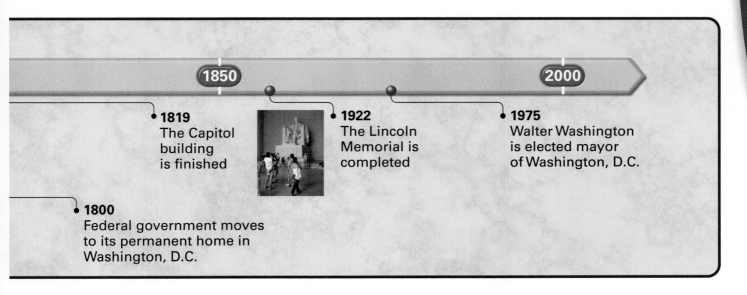

1800
Federal government moves to its permanent home in Washington, D.C.

1819
The Capitol building is finished

1850

1922
The Lincoln Memorial is completed

1975
Walter Washington is elected mayor of Washington, D.C.

2000

Chart and Graph Skills

Lesson 3

Equal Rights for All

What to Know
How did people work toward equal rights for all Americans?

Vocabulary
amendment p. 107
prejudice p. 107
civil rights p. 108

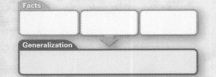

Generalize

The Lincoln Memorial. The Washington Monument. The Capitol. The National Mall. All these places have great meaning to the people of the United States. They are symbols of the democratic ideas on which our country was founded. People have come to these places to talk about freedom and equality. These people have inspired others to work for change.

"Let us ... bind up the nation's wounds ... to do all which may achieve ... a just and lasting peace among ourselves and with all nations." — Abraham Lincoln, 1865

"Where any one class is made to feel that society is [a] conspiracy to ... oppress, rob, and degrade them, neither persons nor property will be safe."
— Frederick Douglass, 1886

Working for Equal Rights

In 1865, when Abraham Lincoln became President for the second time, he gave a famous speech in front of the Capitol. Lincoln talked about peace after the Civil War and the end of slavery in the United States.

Over time, **amendments**, or changes, have been added to the Constitution to give people more rights. One amendment made slavery illegal. Other amendments gave people the rights to vote and own land and the right to an education. Even so, some groups often faced prejudice (PREH•juh•duhs). **Prejudice** is the unfair treatment of a person because of his or her background, race, or religion.

Frederick Douglass spent much of his life working for the equal treatment of African Americans and other groups. In 1894, Douglass spoke at the Metropolitan AME Church in Washington, D.C. He wanted leaders to make laws to protect the rights of African Americans.

Reading Check ☼**Generalize**
How did Frederick Douglass work for equal rights?

The Civil Rights Movement

A Civil Rights movement grew in the 1960s. **Civil rights** are rights that give everyone equal treatment under the law. People came to Washington, D.C., to give speeches, march in parades, and join protests. They were letting the government know that they wanted all people to be treated fairly.

Dr. Martin Luther King, Jr.

On August 28, 1963, more than 250,000 people gathered at the Lincoln Memorial. They listened to Dr. Martin Luther King, Jr., talk about his hopes for equality in the United States. Dr. King's speech inspired change. In 1964, Congress passed the Civil Rights Act. This law says that all Americans have the right to use public places and services. It also says that employers cannot refuse to hire people because of their race, religion, or gender.

"I have a dream that my four little children will one day live in a nation where they will not be judged by the color of their skin, but by the content of their character." — Dr. Martin Luther King, Jr., 1963

Poor People's March

In 1968, people came to the Poor People's March on the National Mall. They wanted better living conditions for the nation's poor. Civil rights leader Rodolfo Gonzales attended the march. He wanted jobs, good housing, and education for Mexican Americans.

Reading Check ⚙ **Generalize**
What was the Civil Rights movement?

Summary People can make changes. They can give speeches and lead marches. This effort is how people won civil rights. Important events in the Civil Rights movement took place in Washington, D.C.

"No one has the right to oppress the people."
— Rodolfo Gonzales, 1975

Review

1. **What to Know** How did people work toward equal rights for all Americans?

2. **Vocabulary** How are the terms **amendment** and **civil rights** related?

3. **Geography** Where in Washington, D.C., did people march and give speeches?

4. **Critical Thinking** Why was Washington, D.C., a center for speeches, parades, and protests during the Civil Rights movement?

5. 🖌 **Illustrate a Bulletin Board** Listen to Dr. King's "I Have a Dream" speech. Illustrate parts of the speech. Put your drawings on a bulletin board.

6. ⭐(Focus Skill) **Generalize** On a sheet of paper, copy and complete the graphic organizer below.

Facts

Abraham Lincoln, Frederick Douglass, Dr. Martin Luther King, Jr., Rodolfo Gonzales, and others worked for the equal treatment of all people.

Generalization

Biography

Trustworthiness

Respect

Responsibility

Fairness

Caring

Patriotism

Speaking Out for Freedom

Many men and women came to Washington, D.C., to fight for civil rights. Some gave historic speeches in front of thousands of people. Others brought about change through their actions.

Mary Church Terrell did many things that women of her time were not "supposed" to do, such as go to college. Later, she traveled the country giving civil rights speeches. When Terrell was 86 years old, she went to a restaurant in Washington, D.C. The owners only served white people. Terrell was asked to leave because she was African American. She said this order broke the law. The Supreme Court agreed with Terrell. In 1953, it ordered Washington, D.C.'s, restaurants and other public places to serve all people, regardless of their race.

Mary Church Terrell

1863–1954

Character Trait: Fairness

Justin Dart, Jr.
1930–2002
Character Trait: Caring

At the age of 18, Justin Dart became sick with polio. He survived the disease but had to use a wheelchair. For much of his life, Dart worked for the rights of people with disabilities. He helped bring about the Americans with Disabilities Act. President George W.H. Bush signed the act into law in 1990. During the signing, Dart sat beside the President on the White House lawn.

In 1894, at the age of 77, Elizabeth Cady Stanton gave a speech in Washington, D.C. She said that women should have the right to vote. For more than 40 years, Stanton had been giving similar speeches. Her strong beliefs inspired others to join the fight for woman's suffrage.

Elizabeth Cady Stanton
1815–1902
Character Trait: Respect

Why Character Counts

1. How did Mary Church Terrell stand up for fairness?
2. How did Justin Dart demonstrate caring?
3. How did Elizabeth Cady Stanton show respect for women's rights?

 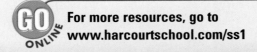 For more resources, go to
www.harcourtschool.com/ss1

Time

Visual Summary

1634
European settlers arrive in the area that is now Washington, D.C.

1783
Americans win independence from Britain.

1791
Pierre L'Enfant designs the capital city.

—— Summarize the Unit ——

Generalize Complete the graphic organizer to make a generalization about the history of Washington, D.C.

Facts

Generalization

Important events shaped Washington, D.C., into the unique, multicultural city that it is today.

Vocabulary

Write a definition for each term.

1. **nomad**, p. 91

2. **colony**, p. 92

3. **independence**, p. 95

4. **survey**, p. 96

5. **civil war**, p. 98

6. **amendment**, p. 107

7. **prejudice**, p. 107

8. **civil rights**, p. 108

1800 1900 2000

1814
British soldiers burn parts of Washington, D.C.

1960
The Civil Rights movement grows.

1974
Walter Washington is elected the first mayor of Washington, D.C.

TEST PREP

 ## Facts and Main Ideas

Answer these questions.

9. What Native American group once lived along the Potomac River?

10. Who designed Washington, D.C.?

11. How did city leaders improve life in Washington, D.C., in the 1870s?

12. Who gave a speech at the Lincoln Memorial about equality in the United States?

Write the letter of the best choice.

13. When did Europeans first settle in the area that is now Washington, D.C.?
    A 1800
    B 1783
    C 1634
    D 1860

14. Which of the following describes a civil rights leader?
    A does not give speeches
    B believes that all people should be treated fairly
    C has prejudice
    D works only in Washington, D.C.

 ## Critical Thinking

15. Why was the capital city located on the Potomac River?

16. Why do people stand up for civil rights?

17. Make it Relevant How are civil rights important to you?

 ## Skills

Read a Time Line

18. Study the time line on pages 104–105. How many years after L'Enfant designed the capital city was the Capitol building finished?

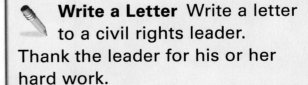 **Write a Story** Imagine living in Washington, D.C., in the early 1800s. Write a story about a day in the city.

Write a Letter Write a letter to a civil rights leader. Thank the leader for his or her hard work.

What's in the explorer's bag?

abc
VOCABULARY

Write the letters that belong in the yellow squares, and you'll know.

1. ☐☐☐☐☐ ☐☐☐
   When citizens of the same country fight each other

2. ☐☐☐☐☐☐
   A place ruled by another country

3. ☐☐☐☐☐
   A person who moves from place to place

4. ☐☐☐☐☐☐☐☐☐☐☐
   Freedom

5. ☐☐☐☐☐☐☐☐
   A change to the Constitution

6. ☐☐☐☐☐☐☐☐
   A kind of Native American building

7. ☐☐☐☐☐ ☐☐☐☐☐☐
   These give everyone equal treatment.

For Your Reference

ALMANAC

GLOSSARY

INDEX

Almanac

FACTS ABOUT WASHINGTON, D.C.

LAND	SIZE	CLIMATE	POPULATION*

 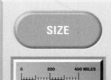  

WASHINGTON, D.C.

Highest Point:
410 feet, in
Northwest D.C.

Lowest Point:
1 foot, along the
Potomac River

Area:
69 square miles

**Greatest
Distance
North/South:**
14 miles

**Greatest
Distance
East/West:**
9 miles

**Average Annual
Temperature:**
53.8° F

**Average Yearly
Rainfall:**
39 inches

**Hottest recorded
temperature:**
106° F, on July 30, 1930

**Coldest recorded
temperature:**
-15° F, on February 11,
1899

Total Population:
550,521*

**Population
Density:**
9,317 people
per square mile

*the most recent
figure available

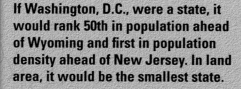

If Washington, D.C., were a state, it would rank 50th in population ahead of Wyoming and first in population density ahead of New Jersey. In land area, it would be the smallest state.

Each year, more than 15 million tourists visit the city's museums and monuments. The most popular museum in Washington, D.C., is also the most popular in the world: The National Air and Space Museum is visited by more than nine million people each year.

GOVERNMENT

WASHINGTON, D.C. SYMBOLS

Mayor: Elected to a four-year term

Council of the District of Columbia: 13 elected members, one from each of the eight wards and five elected at-large.

Congressional Delegation: One non-voting delegate to the U.S. House of Representatives; two shadow senators, and one shadow representative

Advisory Neighborhood Commissions (ANCs): 37 Advisory Neighborhood Commissions study issues affecting the District's neighborhoods

Motto: *Justitia Omnibus* (Latin, meaning "Justice for all")

Flower: American beauty rose

Bird: Wood thrush

At 555 feet tall, the Washington Monument is among the world's tallest stone structures.

Massachusetts Avenue is the longest street in Washington, D.C., and the only one to run through three quadrants.

Every day, about $30 million in paper money is printed at the Bureau of Engraving and Printing in Washington, D.C.

Almanac R3

Glossary

The Glossary contains important history and social science words and their definitions, listed in alphabetical order. Each word is respelled as it would be in a dictionary. When you see this mark ´ after a syllable, pronounce that syllable with more force. The page number at the end of the definition tells where the word is first used in this book. Guide words at the top of the pages help you quickly locate the word you need to find.

add, āce, câre, pälm; end, ēqual; it, īce; odd, ōpen, ôrder; tŏŏk, pool; up, bûrn; yoo as u in fuse; oil; pout; ə as a in above, e in sicken, i in possible, o in melon, u in circus; check; ring; thin; this; zh as in vision

A

absolute location, (ab•sə•loot´ lō•kā´shən) The exact location of a place. p. 8

ambassador, (am•ba´sə•dər) A representative to another country. p. 44

amendment, (ə•mend´mənt) A change to the Constitution. p. 107

B

barter, (bär´tər) To trade without using money. p. 70

C

canal, (kə•nal´) A human-made waterway. p. 15

citizen, (sit´ə•zən) A person who lives in and belongs to a community. p. 54

civil rights, (si´vəl rīts) The rights that give everyone equal treatment under the law. p. 108

civil war, (si´vəl wôr) A war in which people of the same country fight each other. p. 98

climate, (klī´mət) The kind of weather a place has over a long time. p. 12

colony, (kä´lə•nē) A place ruled by another country. p. 92

commission, (kə•mi´shən) A group that meets for a special purpose. p. 51

committee, (kə•mi´tē) A group of people who work together to study and report on certain city problems. p. 56

Constitution, (kän•stə•too´shən) The plan of government for the whole country. p. 40

continent, (kän´tə•nənt) One of the seven largest land areas on Earth. p. 5

council, (koun´səl) A group that meets to make laws. p. 50

E

equator, (i•kwā´tər) An imaginary line which divides Earth into the Northern and Southern Hemispheres. p. 5

F

Fall Line, (fôl līn) The point where hilly land and flat land meet, and rivers drop from higher to lower land. p. 11

federal, (fe´də•rəl) Having to do with the national government. p. 40

G

good, (gŏŏd) A thing that can be bought or sold. p. 68

H

hearing, (hir´ing) A special meeting at which city leaders listen to the people. p. 56

hemisphere, (he´mə•sfir) One half of Earth. p. 5

history map, (his´tə•rē map) A map that shows you how a place looked during an earlier time period. p. 22

human feature, (hyoo´mən) Things that people add to a place. p. 14

I

immigrant, (i´mi•grənt) A person who has moved from another country to live. p. 17

independence, (in•də•pen´dəns) Freedom. p. 95

J

jury, (jŏŏ´rē) A group of citizens who attend a trial and then decide whether the person on trial has broken a law. p. 57

lines of latitude, (līnz əv laˊtə•tood) A set of lines that run east and west on a map or globe. They measure the distance in degrees north or south of the equator. p. 8

lines of longitude, (līnz əv länˊjə•tood) A set of lines that run north and south on a map or globe. They measure the distance in degrees east or west of the prime meridian. p. 8

longhouse, (lôngˊhous) A type of Native American building that is long, narrow, and has a curved roof. p. 90

manufacturing, (man•yə•fakˊchə•ring) To make products using machines. p. 74

memorial, (mə•môrˊē•əl) Something that helps keep the memory of a person or an event alive. p. 26

monument, (mänˊyə•mənt) A structure built to honor an important person or event. p. 26

municipal, (myoo•niˊsə•pəl) Having to do with a city. p. 48

need, (nēd) A thing people must have to live. p. 66

nomad, (nōˊmad) A person who moved from place to place hunting and gathering. p. 91

opportunity cost, (ä•pər•tooˊnə•tē kôst) What is given up in order to get another item when trading. p. 82

physical feature, (fiˊzi•kəl fēˊchər) A feature of a place, including its landforms, waterways, climate, and plant life. p. 10

plantation, (plan•tāˊshən) A large farm. p. 73

prejudice, (preˊjə•dəs) The unfair treatment of a person because of his or her background, race, or religion. p. 107

prime meridian, (prīm mə•riˊdē•ən) An imaginary line which divides Earth into the Western and Eastern Hemispheres. p. 8

Q

quadrant, (Kwäˊdrənt) A part of an area that is divided into four sections. p. 7

R

recreation, (re•krē•āˊshən) Any activity that people do for fun. p. 78

relative location, (reˊlə•tiv lō•kāˊshən) Where a place is in relation to one or more places on Earth. p. 6

responsibility, (ri•spon•sə•bilˊə•tē) A duty, or something a person must do because it is important. p. 55

S

services, (sərˊvə•səs) The work people do for others for money. p. 68

specialize, (speˊshə•līz) To make or sell one kind of product or service. p. 69

suburb, (subˊərb) A smaller town near a city. p. 20

survey, (sûrˊvā) To mark. p. 96

T

tax, (taks) The money citizens pay to the government. p. 79

time line, (tīmˊ līn) A diagram that shows when and in what order events took place. p. 104

tourism, (toorˊiz•əm) The selling of goods and services to tourists. p. 75

trade-off, (trādˊôf) The giving up of one thing to get something else. p. 82

transportation, (trans•pər•tāˊshən) Ways to move from one place to another. p. 78

V

veteran, (veˊtə•rən) A person who fought in a war. p. 26

GLOSSARY

Index

The Index lets you know where information about important people, places, and events appear in the book. All key words, or entries, are listed in alphabetical order. For each entry, the page reference indicates where information about that entry can be found in the text. Page references for illustrations are set in italic type. An italic *m* indicates a map. Page references set in boldface type indicate the pages on which vocabulary terms are defined. Related entries are cross-referenced with *See* or *See also*. Guide words at the top of the pages help you identify which words appear on which page.

See also President
of municipal government,
50. *See also* City council;
Mayor
of state government, 42

Factories, 74, *74*
Factors of production, *68*
Fairness, 110
Fall Line, 11, 13
Falls of the Potomac, *10–11*,
11, 15
Farming. *See* Agriculture
(farming)
Federal government, 40, *40*, 41,
41, 44. *See also* Congress;
President; Supreme Court
Fenty, Adrian, *44, 55*
Field trips
National Mall, 30–31, *30*,
m30, 31
White House, 46–47, *46*,
m46, 47
Fire department, 77
Fishing, 92
Flags, 48, *48*
Flour mills, 74
Frederick Douglass House,
m19, 29
Freedom(s)
of citizens, 55–56
protection of, 39, 54
speaking out for, 106–109,
110–111, *110, 111*
Friendship Arch, *17*
Fun with Social Studies, 34,
62, 86, 114

Garbage collection, *76*, 77
Generalize, 28, 71, 77, 91, 93,

95, 97, 99, 101, 107, 109, 112
Georgetown, *14*, 15, *15*
Gonzales, Rodolfo, 109, *109*
Goods, 65, 68
Government, 38–62
branches of, *41*, 42, 50
city, 43, *43*, 48–53
county, 43
democratic, 54
early businesses and, 73
federal, 40, 41, *41*, 44. *See
also* Congress; President;
Supreme Court
levels of jurisdiction of, *40*
local, 43, *43*. *See also* Cities,
government of; County
government
municipal, 37, 43, *43*, 48–53
reasons for, 38, 39
services provided by, 39, 41,
42, 43, 76–79, *76, 77*
state, 40, 42, *42*
town, 43
working together, 44
Government buildings, 25, *25*.
*See also individual building
names*
Governor, 42
Great Britain. *See* Britain

Health and safety, 39, *39*, 43,
77
Hearing, 56
Hemispheres, 4, *4*, 5
**Hispanic Americans, civil
rights of,** 109, *109*
Historical sites, 29, *29*
History maps, 22–23, *m22*,
m23, 33
House(s), *15*, 88, 90, *90*
House of Representatives.
See Congress

Howard University, 16
Human features, 3, 14, *15*
Hunting and gathering, 91

Immigrants, 17
Income tax, 79
Independence, 95
Indians. *See* Native Americans
Iwo Jima Memorial, 26

J

Japanese cherry trees, 12, *12*
Jefferson, Thomas, 26
Jefferson Memorial, *25*, 26, 100
J.E. Hanger factory, 74
**John A. Wilson Municipal
Building,** *51*
Judicial branch
of municipal government,
50
of national government, *41*,
110. *See also* Supreme
Court
of state government, 42
Jury, 37, 57

K

Kelly, Sharon Pratt, 53, *53*
King, Dr. Martin Luther, Jr.,
108, *108*
Korean War Memorial, 26, *27*,
m27

Landscape, 10–13, *10–11, 12*
Latinos, civil rights of, 109,
109
Latitude, 8–9, *m8, m9*

INDEX

careful reading of the index